LIBERALS & OTHER BORN-AGAIN CHRISTIANS

LIBERALS & OTHER BORN-AGAIN CHRISTIANS

*Many Minds,
One Heart*

Sally B. Geis

ABINGDON PRESS
Nashville

LIBERALS & OTHER BORN-AGAIN CHRISTIANS:
MANY MINDS, ONE HEART

Copyright © 1997 by Abingdon Press

This book is printed on recycled, acid-free, elemental-chlorine–free paper.

Library of Congress Cataloging-in-Publication Data

Geis, Sally B., 1928-
    Liberals and other born-again Christians :   many minds, one heart /
Sally B. Geis.
        p. cm.
    Includes bibliographical references.
    ISBN 0-687-01797-1 (pbk. : alk. paper)
    1. Christian ethics—United States.   2. Liberalism (Religion)—United States.
    I. Title.
BJ1251.G38 1997
277.3'0829—DC21   97-22742
                                                                      CIP

97 98 99 00 01 02 03 04 05 06—10 9 8 7 6 5 4 3 2 1

*To Bob
whose life is a lesson
in patience and respect*

CONTENTS

ACKNOWLEDGMENTS

Some persons believe it takes a village to raise a child. I know it takes a community to write a book. A lifetime of lay participation in Protestant churches laid the foundation upon which this book rests. The faith of my Christian educator mother and physician father formed the core. Other bricks were laid by dedicated but unheralded church school teachers, clergy, women's society members, choir directors, organists, youth workers and scores of other loyal church members whose resilience and commitment have undergirded my love and concern for the church.

The courage to express my convictions about the needs of the contemporary church was nurtured by current colleagues in two different settings. Donald E. Messer, president of the Iliff School of Theology is mentor as well as colleague. Without his support the project would never have become reality. Ruth L. Fuller, M.D., psychiatrist and research partner in the psychiatry department of the University of Colorado Health Sciences Center, sharpened my observation skills and motivated me to express some of the analysis contained in the book. My husband, adult children, and grandchildren offered the personal encouragement one needs to persevere throughout the project.

Numerous friends accepted the thankless task of reading manuscript. Their critiques were invaluable. Harvey C. Martz, Eulalie Hartman, George Tinker, Ruth L. Fuller, Donald E. Messer, Robert B. Geis, and Paula R. Johnston critiqued the work from a variety of perspectives. Suzanne

Calvin provided expertise in editing the first draft. Paul Millette provided crucial library research skill. Virginia Culver, *Denver Post* religion writer, also offered valuable research assistance. Maggie Roe, as student assistant, worked tirelessly with the details. Revel Loedy and Alberta Smith provided essential secretarial support with patience and good cheer. Marti Zimmerman, director of the Iliff Institute for Lay and Clergy Education, graciously indulged me by offering resources from the Institute office. Mary Ruth Howes, manuscript editor, gave essential guidance and counsel. To each of these persons I extend my heartfelt thanks. However, responsibility for the final product is mine alone.

LIBERALS & OTHER BORN-AGAIN CHRISTIANS

INTRODUCTION

Can We All Be Born Again?

"Nowhere else in the world do you have to be a right-wing conservative to be considered a born-again Christian. This is a uniquely American aberration."[1] My objections to the aberration motivated the title of this book. Christians of all ideological persuasions believe in the transformative power of God's message to humankind. So I invite fundamentalists, liberals, evangelicals, and secularists drawn toward Christianity's moral and ethical tenets to use these commentaries on the contemporary church as incentives for institutional and individual transformation.

Most of us, regardless of our ideological label, share "a vague but strong sense that what's going wrong in American life isn't just about economics. It also entails an ethical or moral crisis."[2] I am not offering a recipe for a grand religious reformation, if reformation is defined as a resuscitation of past church life. I am offering some modest suggestions about solutions to several major predicaments facing organized churches and their members. "Modest" means that none of the suggestions cost money or require the development of a new committee. Most require changes in perspective rather than changes in structure or policy. Mental health professionals who seek to help troubled persons change their lives for the better believe, "The keystone of transformation is understanding."[3] This principle hints at a far more profound statement that has deeper meaning, a biblical statement that goes to the heart of the Christian message. "Jesus answered him [Nicodemus], 'Truly, truly, I say to you, unless one is born anew, he cannot see the kingdom of God' " (John 3:3).

13

The dilemmas I have chosen for analysis represent my judgment about which issues currently seem most confusing to the average church participant. They include: perspectives on Christian values, with particular emphasis on reasons why liberal values no longer dominate American public policy debate; an educated guess about whether the internal religious conflict between conservatives and liberals can be resolved; analysis of the contribution white people make to American's escalating racial tensions; comments on the advisability of restructuring denominational institutions in order to recapture what churches have lost. A final chapter addresses the overarching question implied throughout the book: Can the lives of contemporary American Christians be transformed into a more hopeful and vibrant influence on the communities and cultures in which we live?

WHOEVER ASKS THE QUESTIONS CONTROLS THE ANSWERS

A colleague with whom I team-taught a number of courses began each class by emphasizing the importance of asking the right question. "How one approaches a problem is of crucial importance to the success of the analysis," she used to say. "Ask a profound question and the answers will have substance. Ask a superficial question and the answer will be mediocre at best."[4] She spent more time challenging students to improve the quality of their questions than helping them find the answers. Her perspective on critical analysis was the most valuable legacy her students received.

The same philosophy prevails in this book. The goal is to help American Christians improve the quality of our questions about religious renewal. Any set of questions has limitations, since none of us sees the whole of God's meaning in the world. Each of us is blind to some concerns as well as to some insights that are of crucial importance to another person. The success of this book depends on how well it stimulates readers to develop new and better questions for themselves. Solving the problems within American church and society requires careful thought and insight from each of us.

WHO IS ASKING THESE QUESTIONS?

The questions asked in this book come from the perspective of an aging, liberal, mainline laywoman who is white and upper middle class. White middle-class men still dominate church leadership. White women represent the next largest group of leaders. This viewpoint does not represent the outlook of the numerical majority of Christians worshiping today. That majority lives outside the United States, is not white, and most are not over fifty years of age. Unfortunately, my perspective, except for gender, represents the social location of a large majority of the decision makers in American Christian churches, both conservative and liberal; fundamentalist, evangelical, or mainstream.

HOW DO WE KNOW WE HAVE A PROBLEM?

Those of us who have sat in the pews of mainline churches for most of our lives sense that something has gone wrong in our churches as well as within our society at large. Furthermore, we fear that whatever is wrong may be getting worse. Yet when we ordinary church citizens try to understand what has happened and what we might do to make things better, the task seems so complex that we often feel like giving up. Can we understand better and move beyond our worries to adequate solutions? Perhaps this book will help us do just that.

What are the signs of trouble? Are there any signs of hope? Membership is down. On the other hand the rate of membership loss has slowed.[5] Our prestige in the secular world has eroded. In the 1950s and 1960s when someone referred to a political candidate as a God-fearing man we took it for granted that the person was a Christian and probably a member of a mainline denomination. This no longer seems to be a safe assumption. Scholars, however, disagree about the seriousness of the erosion of mainline power. Some say that mainline Protestants, particularly Episcopalians, Presbyterians, and Congregationalists, are found in far greater proportion in positions of power than any other group in American society. Others suggest that religious pluralism and privatization have eroded the impact of mainline Protestantism in American society.[6] No matter who is correct, we feel less influential, and that makes us uneasy.

Much else has changed. Whether for good or ill depends on your point of view. Liberals think much of the change is good. Women and non-Euro-American persons now have more power in church decision making—not as much as many of us would like, but more than in past decades. Religious pluralism is being accepted as a cultural reality. Some mainline churches have seminars to acquaint members with other faiths including Islam, and even cooperate with congregations of other faiths. Gay men and lesbian women are allowed to protest discriminatory church policies in open forums. Viewed from a conservative perspective, however, many of these changes are dangerous and may well have caused our difficulties.

Some church problems worry all of us, whether we are conservative, liberal, or moderate. The denominational financial picture has changed. More money is being collected than ever before within some denominational bodies, but funds for mission and ministry are eroded by the ever-increasing costs of institutional maintenance—clergy pension, health care plans, and liability insurance, for instance. Furthermore, as Loren Mead reminds us, younger persons are not contributing to religious institutions as generously as did their elders. In a more hopeful tone he also notes that an increasing number of mainline Protestants are practicing tithing and some denominations have experienced remarkable growth of pledged giving.[7]

Some mainline churches have vital programs for children and youth, but our congregations are aging. We wonder where the children are. Many of us are troubled because even our own children and grandchildren do not seem to find our church relevant to their needs. They look to a variety of other sources for spiritual direction and ethical guidance.

Outside the church, America's secular socioeconomic and political analysts have written with increasing frequency about disturbing cultural trends that should be of deep concern to all of us in communities of faith. Peter Drucker reminds us that "no century in recorded history has experienced so many social transformations and such radical ones as the twentieth century."[8] Some of these transformations have gotten a great deal of attention from religious leadership, primarily those relating to the disintegration of traditional families. Disturbing indicators include the increase in one-parent families, more births out of wedlock, more drug-addicted mothers.[9]

Other equally astonishing transformations, however, have drawn little or no attention. For example, economists tell us that the nature of work is changing so radically that even the idea of jobs is becoming obsolete. The reorganization of work is creating unfamiliar risks as well as opportunities.[10] The gap between the rich and the poor is growing at an alarming rate. From 1992 to mid-1995, six CEOs cut 178,000 jobs while tripling their own average compensation from

$1.3 million in 1989 to $4.0 million in 1994.[11] Racial tension is increasing.[12] Scandalous behavior on the part of political, business, and religious leaders has resulted in a precipitous decline in public confidence. In response to a question about whether most people can be trusted, 76 percent of the people answered yes in 1994. Only 35 percent answered yes in 1995.[13] Americans do not trust one another anymore.

We who sit in the Sunday morning pews agree with Jim Wallis: "The world isn't working. Things are unraveling, and most of us know it."[14] Yet we keep coming to church hoping for some answers. What went wrong, not only in the church but in society as a whole? Family life seems to be crumbling; business ethics are deteriorating; media violence bombards us; the environmental crisis worsens—and nothing we try to do as church or society seems to help. Most frightening of all, many of us doubt that the future can be better, no matter how hard we try.

RELIGIOUS RESPONSES—A PARADOX

As I mentioned earlier, some of these concerns have elicited a curious lack of attention from denominational and local church leaders. Sociologists, including Donald A. Luidens, suggest that though churches are deeply affected by these cultural trends, leaders seem to believe that the problems as well as the solutions can be found internally in the denominations themselves. The matters of most concern to church leaders seem to be loss of membership, distrust of denominational bureaucracy, and conflicts over doctrine and theology that focus on the issues of homosexuality, abortion, and the role of women in the church.[15]

Meanwhile some of the most profound concerns addressed by secular social critics seem to claim little attention from the majority of our church analysts. Of course there are exceptions. One thinks immediately of Jim

18

Wallis, Katie Cannon, Cornel West, Rosemary Ruether, Harold Recinos, and a handful of others. These may be our contemporary prophets, but they are not major power brokers in the formulation of denominational policies.

When church leaders discuss this cultural unraveling, the concern most frequently absent from their deliberations is the alienation of the upper and upper middle class from the rest of society. Social analysts are alarmed over the increasing greed, insensitivity, and withdrawal from community life of upper-middle-class persons. Evidence includes not only the widening gap between the rich and the poor but also the lifestyles of the rich. Isolated communities with walls or fenced and guarded gates are springing up across the nation. Resort communities devoted to golf or skiing continue to proliferate. Persons within these communities encounter the poor and the nonwhite segment of our society only as servants. The servants' children seem invisible. Yet this change in American lifestyles receives scant attention in church policy-making circles. The next time you attend a church policy-making session, such as a General Assembly or General Conference, compare the number of speeches made on the sin of homosexuality with the number related to the sin of greed. The fact that church leaders are preoccupied with certain lifestyle issues but not others seems astonishing.

ANSWERS FROM CHURCH LEADERS

Currently most of us see ourselves as good Christians who are trying to be helpful and make life better. One thesis that permeates this book is the conviction that we must shift our focus, change our perspective on the role we are called to play as Christians. Those of us who support institutionalized religion, liberals and conservatives, need to be shaken out of complacency with the way we lead our own lives. We need to focus more on reforming ourselves than on reforming or changing others. Such a transformation cannot take place unless we understand how our middle-class religious identity contributes to the problems we are experiencing. Perhaps if we see our dilemma more clearly, and ask better questions about it, the results of our Christian efforts will be more fruitful.

When church leaders address the problem of moral decline, we hear a discordant chorus of voices offering a disparate variety of answers. Some leaders are convinced that the solution lies in a return to traditional values, to prefeminist scriptural interpretations and to former patterns for family life and work styles. Others believe our problem is too much bureaucracy. We must trim general church agency budgets and give power back to the local church if mainline religion is to be vigorous again.

Most mainline Protestants, however, who are not deeply involved in the politics and structures of the church seem uncertain that either the conservative theological solution or the restructuring solution will cure what ails us. Advocating a return to the past draws mixed reaction. Many of us are proud of our own daughters whom we see raising well-adjusted children while participating in careers. We do not want to send our daughters back to the kitchen. On the other hand, we hear about increases in teenage pregnancy, drug use in elementary schools, and stories of children shooting children. We are appalled. Maybe the church should pressure for the moral conformity of the past, we think. It did seem to result in more family stability, with fewer divorces and teenage pregnancies.

Some leaders suggest that the church is dysfunctional because of its structure. Denominational executives are turning to the literature of business management to discover more satisfactory answers to questions about organizing and marketing religion. The management proponents say we need a "paradigm shift." We must revision, reengineer, or reinvent ourselves as Christian communities. Many denominations are currently developing restructure plans for general church boards and agencies. Workshops abound on how to refocus the local church.

Many of us have attended these workshops or sat on restructure committees. Much of the material is helpful, and many local churches are encouraged by the results they achieve with the new techniques. However, some lay-women and laymen know that management workshops have not created magical transformation in the workplace and probably will not in the church. (Remember when we thought the Japanese system had all the answers?)

During this time of turmoil, as churches struggle to respond better, too many of us find ourselves relating to our churches in much the same way the American public current-ly relates to its government. We react with disinterest, alien-ation and even distrust. The bitter struggle between conserva-tive and liberal factions of the faith alienates us further. These acrimonious debates drain our energy. We are discouraged by the amount of energy and time Christians spend on infight-ing, and we wonder what happened to Christian charity.

However, the bitterness of insider disagreements among Christians is not the only discouraging issue. Like our gov-ernment, the institutional church seems both paralyzed and preoccupied with bureaucratic matters that strike some of us as irrelevant to the purpose of the church. In our disillu-sionment, some of us finally turn away in disgust.

ASKING BETTER QUESTIONS

If we look more carefully, however, we may find that the reality of our situation is not as dark as it seems. There is hope. But as one Christian who has not given up on the church said recently, "Something about us doesn't want hope, is threatened by Easter. Hope dislocates us, robs us

21

of our cherished alibis."[16] Those of us who are genuinely committed to our worshiping communities of faith cannot allow our alibis to remove us from the turmoil.

Against this backdrop of confusion and concern, hope and commitment, we begin our analysis of specific issues. Each chapter concludes with a summary that returns us to our overarching question: Can transformation occur? Can all of us who call ourselves Christian be born again into new ways of seeing and behaving?

In chapter 1 we turn our attention to the first topic for analysis, a topic that receives wide attention in the secular world as well as the religious world: Christian values.

FOR REFLECTION

1. What does being born again mean to you? Recall an example from your own life experience or the experience of someone you know.

2. Can you recall a time when you wer upset or angry about the way somebody else used the phrase "born again"?

3. In the next ten years, do you think your local church will become stronger or weaker?

NOTES

1. Tom Sine in *Context: a commentary on the interaction of religion and culture,* edited by Martin Marty (Chicago: Claretian Publications, vol. 28, no. 15), August 15, 1996, p. 1. The quotation originally appeared in *Prism* and again in *Other Side,* May-June 1996.

2. E. J. Dionne, Jr., "Morality is a workplace issue, too," *The Denver Post,* March 25, 1996, p. 7B.

3. I am indebted to Ruth L. Fuller, M.D., psychiatrist and Christian, who crystallized this insight with the quoted words in a private conversation.

4. Lucy B. Creighton was professor of economics at Colorado Women's College, Denver, Colorado.

5. "Membership Decline Slows Further," *United Methodist Reporter,* August 4, 1995, p. 1.

6. Gustav Spohn, "Study: Mainline Protestants Still Pack a Punch," *United Methodist Reporter,* December 30, 1994, p. 1.

7. Loren B. Mead, "O Sacred Immovables: Confronting the Barriers to Change and Growth," *In Trust*, Summer 1995, pp. 13-14.

8. Peter Drucker, "The Age of Social Transformation," *The Atlantic Monthly*, November 1994, p. 53.

9. For an interesting analysis of the disintegration see Richard Whitmire, "1987: Was it the year that things started going wrong in U.S.?" *The Denver Post*, February 27, 1994, pp. 21A, 24A.

10. William Bridges, "The End of the Job," *Fortune*, September 19, 1994, pp. 62-74. See also Robert Reich, *The Work of Nations* (New York: Alfred A. Knopf, 1991).

11. S. McNaughton,"CEO Salaries Rise as Jobs Are Lost," *Boston Globe Graphic*, reprinted in *The Denver Post*, February 18, 1996.

12. *Rocky Mountain News*, Sunday, November 12, 1995. Poll results to the question, "Thinking about race relations in the 1990s, are things in this country improving, staying about the same or getting worse?" Improving 13.5%, Same 32.2%, Worse 52.9%.

13. Richard Morin and Dan Balz, "Americans Losing Trust in Each Other and Institutions," *The Washington Post*, January 28, 1996, p. A1.

14. Jim Wallis, *The Soul of Politics*, A Harvest Book (San Diego: Harcourt Brace & Co., 1995), p. xiii.

15. Donald A. Luidens quoted by Clifton F. Guthrie in a review of Jackson Carroll and Wade Clark Roof, *Beyond Establishment: Protestant Identity in a Post-Protestant Age* (Louisville: Westminster/John Knox Press, 1993), in *Quarterly Review*, Fall 1994, p. 339.

16. William Willimon "Learning to Love the Local," *Circuit Rider*, May 1995, p. 5.

CHAPTER ONE

Why Liberals Can't Market Their Values

For several decades values seemed irrelevant to secular decision making. Today, however, we find ourselves in a sociopolitical culture more concerned about values than about anything else. The interest in Christian values, as well as the depth of the conflicted discussion surrounding some of them, puzzles many of us who hold membership in churches. Much of the debate focuses on deciding whether conservatives or liberals represent a correct interpretation of scripture. Since persons on both sides hold strong convictions and are not likely to change their views, this tedious exercise aimed at producing winners and losers seems unproductive. Asking a different question about the values debate may be more fruitful. Perhaps we need to ask why liberal values seem less popular in today's public debate than conservative ones.

THE VALUE CONFLICT DESCRIBED

Though the values in question are often referred to as "family values," much of the conflict focuses on a small number of lifestyle issues. Other values traditionally associated with the Judeo-Christian tradition cause little or no conflict. Efforts to promote honesty, integrity, and kindness seem to please everyone. Christians should remember this broad area of agreement and take comfort in the amount of consensus we can muster.

The disagreement over Christian values, often referred to as family values, pits conservative Christians against a hostile culture that includes secular humanists, non-Christians of almost any persuasion, as well as liberal Christians who do not accept their definitions. On numerous occasions the controversy has erupted into violence. The quarrel over women's right to abortion has resulted in the deaths of physicians and assistants in legal abortion clinics. The controversy over homosexual rights has resulted in legal battles. In some states legislation has been proposed to waive civil rights protection for gay and lesbian persons. Colorado passed a constitutional amendment excluding gay and lesbian persons from protection under civil rights legislation. The amendment was later ruled unconstitutional by the U.S. Supreme Court.[1] Many of us who belong to churches wonder how this predicament came to be. Understanding the nature of social change helps us find the answer.

THE NATURE OF CHANGE

Social theorists teach that within societies composed primarily of persons whose backgrounds are similar, consensus about values and rules for proper behavior is easy to achieve. Minority opinions are easily suppressed or may even be overlooked. However, as the composition of a society changes so that its makeup is more diverse, consensus becomes increasingly difficult to achieve. America's growing diversity suggests that achieving consensus about values will become increasingly difficult. If we view consensus as a utopian ideal, rather than a viable option, we can ask a more realistic question. Can we live together peacefully when we do not agree? (Part of the answer comes in the next chapter.)

THE ROLE OF RELIGION

When consensus within a society disintegrates, members are bound to ask, Whose job is it to hold things together? Sociologists have long viewed religious institutions as the primary provider of rules that maintain a cohesive society. The moral code of right and wrong provides not only the rules for behavior but a definition of punishment. David Popenoe once observed that religion works better than any other institution involved in social control (including law enforcement) because "religion . . . offers a more complete or extensive method of controlling deviance . . . it adds a sort of supernatural 'detective' power."[2]

Contemporary cultural and political behavior seems to confirm these assumptions about the role of religion. "Return to Christian values" has become a rallying call for political speeches and legislative policies aimed at putting the unraveling society back together. Unfortunately, if members of the society, even the religious members, cannot agree on values, it becomes almost impossible to turn values into clear-cut rules. If there are no clear-cut rules, how can the society know who violates them?

In spite of the enormous difficulty that building consensus presents, most members of this society agree that rules need to be clearer and somebody should be punished for getting our country in such bad shape. But who? Is it welfare mothers, gay and lesbian activists, the media, or greedy corporate stockholders? Everybody has a pet list of offenders, but as a society we cannot seem to agree on where to place the blame.

Without consensus the power of institutionalized religion diminishes, as does the effectiveness of other social controls, including legal controls. At the beginning of 1996, one out of every 167 Americans was in prison or jail. Our country incarcerates more persons than any other nation in the world except Russia, whose rate is about the same as ours. And we want to build more prisons because so many of us feel threatened by rule breakers whom we want to punish![3] Many persons reason that the only way Americans, as a body politic, can come to consensus on values is to impose a code of behavior on its citizens. These persons look to institutionalized religion to provide the values and rules for the code that will, if implemented, glue society back together.

Liberal Christians need to understand that members of the religious right have correctly identified the mood of the nation. There is a call for a more cohesive set of values than our society currently possesses. The religious right's emphasis on strict conformity to certain laws perceived as biblically based fits well with this mood. Hence the popularity of their call for a constitutional amendment forbidding abortion, and for legislation to exclude homosexuals from the protection of civil rights statutes. Most liberals, however, including liberal Christians, see this merger of church values and state control as dangerous.

A LIBERAL VIEW OF VALUES AND RULES

Liberals concur with Howard Becker's explanation of the ways in which values become rules used to punish offenders. In his book *The Outsiders,* Becker, a pioneer social theorist, made several important observations. He pointed out that wrong behavior can only be identified and punished when somebody with power decides which behaviors are wrong.[4] Becker used the terms *insider* and *outsider* to define rule-makers and rule-breakers in social systems. Insiders make the rules. Outsiders are punished for not following them.

Becker's greatest contribution may well have been his observation that most insiders find it to their advantage to follow the rules, since the rules are designed to reward their behavior. Most outsiders do not follow the rules because following them seems to bring little or no reward.[5] To illustrate: In today's world we middle-class insiders condemn inner-city men and boys for selling drugs instead of making a living by engaging in honest employment. However, numerous studies have shown that black inner-city males have never had much success finding employment that pays a living wage.[6] Therefore, lack of employment opportunities may be the principal reason they turn to drug traffic as a rewarding way to make a living. If this is the case, the most effective solution to the drug problem may be creating good paying jobs for inner-city men, not punishing them for breaking the rules.

However, I am not asking readers to take sides about whether punishment or rehabilitation is the better solution to inner-city drug trafficking. That would be to miss the point of this chapter. We live in a pluralistic society where some persons favor one solution and other persons advocate different options. Situations where honest persons disagree about the proper course of action make liberal Christians cautious about granting any one religious or political perspective the privilege of dominating the value debate and demanding conformity. In a pluralistic society, liberal Christians consider it risky to elevate any one set of values into rules that demand conformity of personal behaviors and lifestyles.

This does not mean that liberals are neutral. All Christians, as well as non-Christians, want to make an impact on the contemporary values debate. Recently *USA Today* reporter Patricia Edmonds pointed out that almost every state has passed some type of "values" law in the 1990s. She quotes William Pound, executive director of the National Conference of State Legislatures, who says that where "value laden laws once originated mostly in legislatures' conservative wings or religious caucuses, today they're being offered by a more varied coalition of law-makers."[7] Liberal Christians affirm the process when the debate is open to all. However, some of the legislation itself, such as laws that restrict women's right to choose an abortion, is less pleasing, because it demands conformity. The most perplexing question liberals face in this situation is really a paradox. As society becomes more and more diverse, the liberals' stance that affirms diversity is not widely accepted. Liberals wonder why. Their perplexity stems, in part, from a lack of understanding about the legitimate yearning for a significant degree of consensus. Maintaining a society cohesive enough to function as one body politic demands such consensus.

LIBERAL CHRISTIAN VALUES DESCRIBED

Since consensus about values seems to elude us, a clear description of liberal Christians' family values is in order. The short list covers seven of the value topics debated in the contemporary Christian church as well as in the culture at large. It does not cover all values, just those in greatest contention. Conservatives beware, the list may anger you, but please do not quit reading. If you persevere you will find sharp criticism of the mainline, liberal perspective, as well as its defense.

1. Abortion. Liberals believe that though abortion is always a choice made under less than ideal circumstances, it can be made by a Christian person or family as a reasonable and responsible decision. This conviction cannot be divorced from other closely related issues, such as advocacy for adequate prenatal and postnatal health care, as well as satisfactory child care for working mothers.

2. Sex education, including information about safe sex. Nearly half a century ago my father, who was an obstetrician, said that people do not die from too much accurate

30

information about sexual and reproductive matters. They die from a lack of information. It is imperative that all young people learn about sexually transmitted diseases, the proper use of condoms, the risks of teenage pregnancy.

3. Homosexuality. Liberal Christians favor unconditional acceptance of all persons. Sexual orientation or practice (heterosexual or homosexual), judged out of context and unrelated to a person's moral conduct, is irrelevant. Abusive sex, whether homosexual or heterosexual is deplorable and should never be condoned. Gay unions, sometimes referred to as gay marriages, are legitimate contracts.

4. Divorce. Though divorce is far more acceptable than it once was, there are still sizable groups of Christians who do not find it an acceptable choice for people of the faith. Divorce, like abortion, ruptures the fabric of families, but some circumstances make it acceptable as a responsible Christian course of action. When divorce does occur, careful attention must be paid to the needs of children involved.

5. Gender equality. Christians are advocates for the powerless. In our society, gender, like race and age, can impede access to power. Liberals affirm equal pay for equal work and parental leave for parents of newborn or newly adopted children. We encourage churches to use gender-free language when speaking about God.

6. Affirmative action. Persistent racism demands special attention to laws that guarantee opportunities for education and employment to persons who are not of white, Anglo-Saxon heritage. Liberal Christians support affirmative action to promote equal opportunity.

7. Immigration policy. Our Christian obligation to welcome the stranger leads liberals to defend government policies that provide education, health and social services to the children of illegal immigrants. Children should not be required to live in illness and ignorance.

WE ARE OUR OWN WORST ENEMY

At the beginning of this chapter I posed the question, Why can't liberals market their values? There are a number of possible answers. My analysis makes use of Becker's *insiders* and *outsiders* concept, including his observation that outsiders do not follow rules or accept values they do not find rewarding. If we ask why outsiders do not find the values and rules liberals favor rewarding, we can gain useful insights about liberals as well as about the outsiders. The answers we find may lead us to conclude that a critical examination of our own behavior is more useful than either distress over the behavior of other Christians or efforts to force conformity to our point of view.

Liberal Christians will not make much impact on society at large unless we are willing to make some significant changes in the way we go about our task. Liberals' most serious problem in promoting their version of the family values agenda is not, as some would suggest, the opposition of fundamentalist or evangelical Christians; rather it is our own behavior. *We* are our own worst enemy.

WHY LISTEN TO OUTSIDERS?

At least three identifiable groups of persons within our society hold negative judgments about the liberal approach to value questions: some of our own children, nonwhites, and those on the religious right. Their judgments grow out of an accurate, if unfortunate, understanding of the Christian church's historical treatment of families including the interpersonal and sexual dimensions of family life. If we are willing to face these accurate critics, religious and secular, and address their concerns forthrightly, we will enhance our chances of changing the climate of our community of faith and our culture.

32

Liberals need not heed or placate every critic. Some criticisms leveled at liberal Christians are unreasonable and based on prejudice or misunderstanding. Those who accuse us of not taking the Bible seriously, of advocating promiscuity and debauchery, of not caring what happens to children, are leveling unfounded, even irrational, criticism. However, if we dismiss *all* of our critics because *some* appear to be mean-spirited, if not mentally ill, in their distortions of our position, we are in danger of shutting out thoughtful voices whom we should heed. Ignoring these voices may cause us to lose the family values battle in ways we never intended. We may alienate even more persons from the church.

OUTSIDER-INSIDER IMAGES

Let us now look at the outsiders' view of liberal Christian values. The three groups of outsiders we will discuss are defined by the traditional sociological indicators of age, race, and socioeconomic status. All such categories that force individuals into groups are imperfect, for some individuals who fall into each category do not fit the description. However the classification works sufficiently well to provide a useful framework for discussion.

Our own children as outsiders

Let us begin with the biggest group of outsiders whom mainline churches have lost in this generation. They are white, under forty, well educated, upper middle class, more males than females. These contemporary outsiders grew up in families once identified with mainline churches. Contrary to popular opinion, many of them have not left to become fundamentalist or evangelical Christians. When asked about their religious affiliation, many reply that they have none.

Some "prefer to build their own spirituality off a cafeteria line of belief systems . . . a little bit of this, a little bit of that."[8]

If you want to understand this group's image of the Christian church and its values, find a tape of *Saturday Night Live* that features Dana Carvey's popular TV character, the Church Lady. (She made Carvey famous even before he began impersonating President George Bush.) The Church Lady seems to transcend ideological splits within the Christian tradition. I always think of her as Methodist because I recognize her out of my own tradition. Carvey's genius created a character everybody recognizes.

You will remember that the Church Lady was a white female, middle class, and over sixty. Who better stereotypes the Christian church in America? She is a prim, proper, slightly dowdy matron around whom a faint air of judgmentalism and disapproval hangs. She seems quaint and out of touch with "real life," meaning the life most Americans experience at the workplace, in schools or shopping malls, in bars, health clubs and on the streets.

One imagines her to be easily shocked by nudity or "dirty" words. She seems quite sexless herself—a tight, stiff woman to whom affection and humor do not come easily. Her trademark phrase, "Well, isn't that special!" responds to information or opinions she finds distasteful. It verbalizes a hypocritical acceptance of what she has been told, but really means, "The Good Book says I am supposed to love my neighbor, so I show my virtue by talking with inferior people like you. But I do not have to like it."

The Church Lady is recognizable because the portrayal so accurately depicts the attitude of too many Christians. Is she you and I? Do liberals say in one breath that they accept gay people, divorced people, and single teenage mothers but send a double message, "Well, aren't you special?" Are we, like the Church Lady, arrogant enough to assume that the second part of the message, "I'm better than you and really don't like or approve of you," is not understood by the listener?

If significant numbers of divorced persons, homosexual persons, persons with handicapping conditions, as well as others rejected by society, cannot be found in our pews each Sunday, we live in the same hypocritical social isolation as Church Lady. We say we care, but where is the evidence? The company we keep tells more about our stance toward family values than all the pronouncements of all the study committees that national church bureaucracies can fund.

Those of us within the church should never forget that secular outsiders who identify us with the Church Lady came to their understanding experientially. Apparently they have not found the church a safe place to share the pain of finding themselves pregnant at thirteen, being beaten or sexually abused by a spouse, being gay and afraid to admit it for fear of being called queer.

Fairness, generosity, kindness, standing up for what is right even though there may be a cost are characteristics most people, secular persons as well as Christians, identify as moral and ethical. It seems that some of our own children who grew up in liberal mainline churches have not observed any particular connection between church attendance and these moral or ethical behaviors.

We can hardly fault them when we are faced with results such as those from a Lilly-funded study done recently. It found that 52 percent of mainline Protestant adults, a majority, have never donated time to help the poor, hungry, or sick, and that 78 percent have never spent time promoting social justice.[9] The poor, hungry, and sick include the one in five children in our country who live in poverty, most without health care, many without enough to eat. They also include single mothers who are more likely to give birth to underweight infants and the one- or two-parent families who cannot find decent child care for their children while they work to make ends meet. Neglect of families betrays concern for family values. Our own neglect has contributed to the erosion of "family values."

We insiders, who made the Church Lady rules, need to reconsider the meaning of Christian hospitality. In her book *Confronting the Idolatry of Family: A New Vision for the Household of God,* Janet Fishburn reminds us of an unhealthy and unbiblical expectation among many church members. They assume that the primary purpose of the local church is to create "complete self-fulfillment" in the nuclear family life of the members. Frequently this concept of family self-fulfillment becomes part of "a subtle mixture of love of country, family, and God." How easily this attitude slips into idolatry, into a sense of comfort with a homogeneous congregation of happy parents and children who all look alike, think alike, and defend the political and economic status quo. As Fishburn says, "Protestants in America have been dreaming of a Christian America for two hundred years; they have known only a Christianity in which God has been identified with prosperity and family stability."[10] If we persist in this distortion and fail to broaden our understanding of family to include others who are not like us, we are doomed to failure.

Nonwhite outsiders

If the Church Lady image dominates the thinking of baby boomers or Generation X, another image dominates the thinking of the poor and nonwhite members of society. Many of them see churches as the institutions that provide the rationale for the status quo to the powerful. Ever since Constantine aligned Christianity with political power, the church has offered status and privilege to those involved in its maintenance. Today sociology textbooks still list the institutional church as a structure that serves as primary conserver of traditional forms of order within the social system.

Those who feel oppressed by the socioeconomic order frequently identify the church as a full partner in that oppression. Historically the family whose values the church promotes has been white and middle class. For years the white church stood by and watched or even aided in the dissolution of nonwhite families. African American families saw members sold into slavery apart from their spouses, parents, or children. Native American families suffered the forceful removal of children from their families for placement in government schools. There the youngsters were taught to devalue and disavow the traditional culture of their families. Japanese American families were uprooted from their homes and sent to live behind barbed wire in alien territory because the United States was at war with the country from which their families emigrated.

Why should anything the church has to say about family values today make much difference to these families? These critics care little for the pronouncements from our bureaucratic study committees. They are not even greatly impressed with our campaigns of social justice for families. They are less interested in how many free health clinics "we" are willing to fund for "them" than in the redistribution of the country's wealth.

They remember better than we how wealth is distributed. An illustration from Denver fits most other American cities as well. *The Denver Post* a few years ago made front-page news out of some demographic information that we should all know by heart if we care about families. The wealthiest and poorest neighborhoods in Denver are geographically only eight miles apart, but for families they are two quite different worlds. In Sun Valley, the poorest neighborhood, the average income per person per year is $3,150, and 24 percent of the households are headed by women. In Cherry Hills, the wealthiest neighborhood, the per person (not per family but per person) income is $69,560 and only 3 percent of the households are headed by women.[11]

When establishment church folks work to change the rules

of the economic game, poor people will be more impressed with rhetoric about social justice and family values. Most of them doubt that middle-class whites want to redistribute the wealth. Our actions suggest we would rather give to charity than change the rules and equalize the power. Do we really want to understand why life can look so hopeless and lonely for a fourteen-year-old girl that she wants to have a baby so there will be somebody to love her and for her to love?

Our antiseptic, out-of-touch solutions may not work much longer. The poor and the powerless are less and less willing to express gratitude for charity, for the things middle-class whites want to do *for* them. They want to know what we will do *with* them.

Ironically, the image of liberal Christians held by poor people is still the Church Lady with her well-meant but patronizing attitudes coupled with an out-of-touch sense of reality. As Harold Recinos says in *Jesus Weeps,* his poignant book about life in Puerto Rican New York:

> God feels the pain of the mothers of the urban world who bury their children each day in the cemeteries of the nation's cities. God breathes the stale air of forsaken streets that have become home to countless families who have been sent to the margins of society. . . . [This] reality is the aspect of existence that the church must come to examine more closely.[12]

Dare we risk entering this reality, hearing these voices that tell us we must be present with *all* God's children, see *all* humanity as our family? Do we fear such a radical change?

The religious right as outsiders

The third outsider image, that of the religious right, disturbs us the most. As the conflict between liberal and conservative Christians escalates, persons on each side tend to define those on the other side as the enemy. Psychology teaches that our enemies, meaning the individuals or groups who agitate us the most, are frequently those persons or groups who embody some of our own hidden, undesirable characteristics. Their behavior arouses in us our deepest fears. Above all we fear being "found out."

Who are these conservative Christian enemies? Conservative Christians are people who worry about the erosion of so-called "traditional" family values, meaning the values of the homogeneous, nuclear, two-parent family that has dominated the recent history of white, middle-class society. They are the persons whom Tex Sample describes as the folks on the cultural right. This group includes most evangelicals and many mainline church members who do not identify themselves as liberal. They are fearful that the social order they know and understand is faltering, unstable, and changing radically. The world they have known and trusted all of their lives seems to be on the edge of chaos. One characteristic Sample uses to distinguish the people on the cultural right from the mostly younger and more affluent people on the cultural left is their commitment to deferred gratification. They were raised to work hard, sacrifice for the children, save for the future, live cautiously. Respectability is important to them. They are distressed by a new generation that seems to want it all now, particularly young people who spend what they have, don't care about saving money, and do not seem to care what "the neighbors say" about their lifestyles.[13]

It is scandalous to those on the cultural right that liberal mainline church leadership seems supportive of these irresponsible, loose-living people. Liberal seminary professors and pastors, who should be the keepers of the traditional values, now write books, preach, and make speeches that affirm these new ways of thinking. What is the world coming to, conservatives ask, when church leaders cannot be counted on to define boundaries, to hold firmly to the rules that judge certain behavior as unacceptable and other behavior as exemplary? Have these liberals abandoned family values? Most mystifying of all to the conservatives is the liberal mainline attitude toward them. Many are lifelong church members who support the church with their gifts and their presence. Their support seems welcome, but when they voice their distress at some of these actions and attitudes, the liberals tell them, in subtle and not so subtle ways, that if they do not accept all this permissiveness they are stupid bigots. How, they ask, can we be stupid or bigots if the rules we believe in today are the rules we were taught as children in Sunday school? Who told intellectual liberals they have a right to change the rules? Liberals, not conservatives, are the ones who abdicated their Christian responsibility to stand up for the faith. Liberals have surrendered to a satanic, secular culture.

These last criticisms are the hardest for liberal Christians to hear. Our discomfort comes partly from our embarrassment that we may be "found out." We do affirm diversity of lifestyles, but the family the conservatives want to preserve is, after all, the kind of family in which most contemporary liberal Christians grew to adulthood. We, like the conservatives, yearn for our children and grandchildren to experience the same family relationships. Liberals talk about accepting gay families, single parent families, and blended families. However, the image conservatives cling to is the one with which most liberal Christians feel safest.

Does that mean liberals are hypocrites who say one thing and mean another? For some the answer is probably yes. Hypocrisy can be found among all Christians, liberal and conservative. Many obstetricians know conservative Christian patients who vehemently protest abortion rights, but who have secretly had abortions themselves. They, too, fear being found out.

Hypocrisy invades our Christian social justice stance as well as our attitude toward matters of lifestyle. Most white persons, liberal as well as conservative, are afraid to vote for policies that might dismantle the comfortable alliance between God, country, and family of which Fishburn speaks. All of us harbor some fear of the chaos a world of shared power might bring. We also fear the chaos that pluralism brings, with its lack of consensus, safety, and cohesion.

Yet God calls all Christians to be honest, even about our own shortcomings. Each of us, conservative and liberal, must continually question our motivation. How often do we say one thing but do another? God may be disappointed sometimes with the way all Christians behave.

DO WE HEAR THE OUTSIDERS?

Some critics sound less harsh to liberals than others, so that we find it easier to listen to them. Many of our own children are the nonchurch-affiliated, white, middle-class outsiders. We care enough about them to want to hear their concerns. Numbers of liberal white Christians have friends who are not white upon whom they depend. For example, my psychiatrist colleague Ruth Fuller points out the racism and classism in the papers that we write together. She also edits our papers well. Her skin is very dark, her heritage African American. Isabel Lopez, president of Lopez Leadership Services, patiently tries to teach me not to think like a typical, patronizing white liberal. She asks me to quit trying to solve the race problem or the poverty problem or any other problem associated with poor blacks and Latinos/Latinas. Over and over she says, "Sally, we aren't your problem, you are your problem." George Tinker, who often describes his roots by saying, "My father was Osage, my mother was Lutheran," forces me to look honestly at the history of the church and its role in subjugating nonwhite, indigenous persons here and across the globe.

But until this past summer my only impressions of conservative Christians were stereotypical ones formed by watching TV preachers like Jimmy Swaggart and conservative Christians like Tammy Bakker. It was a comfortable way to distance myself.

Then one summer I spent two weeks with a group of evangelicals. It was more stressful than any two weeks spent overseas or in America's ethnic neighborhoods. In those other cross-cultural situations people whose ideologies were like mine could be found. But evangelicals were another matter!

One woman in the group fit all my stereotypes. She was my idea of a southern belle—a tiny little thing with a drawl, blonde hair, and fashionable clothes. She disapproves of homosexuality, abortion, radical feminism. By liberal standards Eulalie (that really is her name),[14] was about as hopeless theologically and ideologically as anyone could be. However, the first obstacle to erode a liberal's prejudice against her was her behavior. When everybody else got tired and cranky, guess who was bright and cheerful as ever, making the best of it, encouraging the rest of us? Eulalie.

Then it came time to ride with urban police on late-night shifts. Who had more experience with life on the streets than any of us? At home Eulalie rides frequently with members of her local police force. Her special training is in domestic violence and sex abuse. It was a shock to discover she had more experience with out-of-control drunk men, battered and raped women, abused children than any of us. She was no Dana Carvey Church Lady.

As we became friends, the judgment words from Matthew 25 came to mind. Could it be I, not Eulalie, who might find myself among the goats saying, "But, Lord, when did I see you hungry or thirsty or a stranger or naked or sick or in prison and did not minister to you?" (see Matt. 25:44).

As mutual respect developed, she was willing to listen to my concerns and my point of view. She stayed several nights in the home of two gay men and learned to care about them and the discrimination they face. She still believes the Bible says homosexuality is a sin, but "for goodness' sake, Sally, it's not the only sin." As she told me recently, "Now when I read in the paper that three homosexuals have been killed in one week I must wonder if it's anybody I know."

Memories of Eulalie came to me when reading these words by Martin Marty, a wise insider analyst of mainline religion:

> Religious organizations are scurrying to provide better networks of control, to minimize temptation, to anticipate troubles, to create a climate in which abuse of all sorts is prevented or dealt with. We may need a heavier dose of Aristotle: more concern for ethos, character, and what makes a good person.[15]

Marty's words are sobering for a couple of reasons. First, because most liberals involved in justice issues are scurriers. His analysis does not give us much affirmation. Some of the scurrying to control abuse is defensible, but some political strategizing is motivated by our need for control.

We must also deal with the second part of Marty's statement. Do we show enough concern for ethos, character, and what makes a good person? How Christian was it to judge Eulalie by her theology and ideology when she taught me so much about being a good person?

43

SUMMARY

Can we liberals be effective in promoting an understanding of family values within the church and the culture at large? Only if we are willing to open ourselves to all the voices, to all the pain in God's human family. Only if we are willing to risk making our own confessions and doing our own penance.

Can we be optimistic about our ability to effect such a transformation? We can if we remember the legion of courageous and affirming persons within the church who are already building a new vision of inclusiveness and understanding for Christian family values. In his book *A Conspiracy of Goodness*, Donald E. Messer recounts the lives of numerous persons, some famous and many unknown, who care deeply for all God's creation. They work with zeal and kindness to become involved in God's liberating love. One chapter focuses on the image of Christians as bridge-builders. It begins with the story of Andrew Parker who was a passenger on a capsized ferryboat. "His family and others were separated from the safety of a small island of metal by a cascade of water. The chasm proved too wide for people to jump over, so Parker stretched his six-foot, three-inch frame into a bridge . . . twenty people escaped safely."[16]

This critique of the family values conflict is intended to encourage each Christian, conservative and liberal, to become a bridge-builder for understanding. What Andrew Parker did was risky and painful, but it was right. Living, as well as speaking, liberal values is also risky and painful. Only when we live out our values as well as speak them will others listen.

In the next chapter we will focus on the conflict itself by asking, Can we disagree in love?

FOR REFLECTION

1. Howard Becker suggested insiders (those in power) make the rules, but it is the outsiders (the powerless) who are punished for not following them. What evidence do you have that his assumption is or is not an accurate description of your church?
2. Who are the insiders in your church and who are the outsiders?
3. What changes might make some of those outsiders feel more like insiders?
4. Do you think there is any truth to the observation that those persons we find most upsetting are those who possess characteristics that we are ashamed of in ourselves?

NOTES

1. On November 3, 1992, Colorado voters passed Amendment 2 with 53.4 percent of the vote. The text of the Amendment is as follows:
"No protected status based on homosexual, lesbian or bisexual orientation. Neither the state of Colorado, through any of its branches or departments, nor any of its agencies, political subdivisions, municipalities or school districts, shall enact, adopt or enforce any statute, regulation, ordinance or policy whereby homosexual, lesbian or bisexual orientation, conduct, practices or relationships shall constitute or otherwise be the basis of or entitle any person or class of persons to have or claim any minority status, quota preference, protected status or claim of discrimination. This section of the Constitution shall be in all respects self-executing."
On May 20, 1996, the U.S. Supreme Court struck down Amendment 2, ruling 6 to 3 that it was unconstitutional. The U.S. Supreme Court found that states cannot ban laws protecting lesbians, gays, or bisexuals from discrimination.
2. David Popenoe, *Sociology,* 2nd ed. (New York: Appleton, Century, Crofts, 1974), p. 417.
3. Michael J. Sniffen, "Number of jailed Americans hits nearly 1.6 million, Justice reports," Associated Press in *The Denver Post,* August 18, 1996, p. 10A. Statistics quoted from a report by the Bureau of Justice Statistics, Justice Department.
4. Howard Becker, *The Outsiders* (New York: Free Press, 1966), pp. 8-9.
5. *Ibid.*
6. For example, see the classic study by Elliot Liebow, chapter 2, "Men and Jobs," *Tally's Corner* (Boston: Little, Brown & Co., 1967), pp. 29-71. The front cover of my copy has a quote from Daniel Patrick Moynihan: "It is nothing short of brilliant—a work of importance. . . ." Thirty years after this initial study was published, Senator Moynihan is still trying to make the same points in Congress that Liebow made in the book.
7. Patricia Edmonds, "States lead the push to pass 'values' laws," *The Denver Post,* August 18, 1996, pp. 36-37A.

45

8. Martin Marty quoted by Michelle Bearden, *Religion Book Line,* August 15, 1996, vol. 1, no. 14, p. 9.

9. *Newscope,* August 27, 1993, p. 1.

10. Janet Fishburn, *Confronting the Idolatry of Family: A New Vision for the Household of God* (Nashville: Abingdon Press, 1991), p. 55.

11. *The Denver Post,* January 3, 1993, pp. A1, A8.

12. Harold J. Recinos, *Jesus Weeps: Global Encounters on Our Doorstep* (Nashville: Abingdon Press, 1992), p. 40.

13. Tex Sample, *U.S. Lifestyles and Mainline Churches: a Key to Reaching People in the 90's* (Louisville: Westminster/John Knox Press, 1990). See chapter 3, "The Cultural Right," pp. 57-95.

14. I am grateful to Eulalie Hartman, a trustee of Conservative Baptist Seminary in Denver, Colorado, for graciously consenting to lend her name to our true story.

15. Martin E. Marty, "What Friends Are For," *Christian Century,* November 4, 1992, pp. 987-88.

16. Donald E. Messer, *A Conspiracy of Goodness* (Nashville: Abingdon Press, 1992), p. 91.

CHAPTER TWO

Can Christians
Disagree in Love?

Respecting One Another in a Polarized
Culture of Violence

FEAR AND ANGER VS. CIVILITY

Today a great sickness ... threatens the social, political and religious institutions ...: the disappearance of civil dialogue, a disdain of those who hold contrary views, an unease with people of another color, a contempt of those whose lifestyles seem to mock our own.... Stephen L. Carter writes ... in his ... book "Integrity," that almost no one ... left or ... right, liberal or conservative, progressive or moderate, evangelical or fundamentalist, is free from its divisive and destructive contagion.... We all are caught up in it.... We all have a stake in standing ... with those who believe that this assault on decency and fairness can be met by a new civility.[1]

This observation by George Mitrovich and Jim Wallis appeared recently in newspapers across the country. Almost daily one encounters similar concerns. It may be a comment about the way we treat one another in traffic jams, the way political candidates speak of each other in the media, or the rudeness of skateboarders on the sidewalks. Sometimes the expressed concern goes deeper; sometimes we admit to being genuinely afraid of the people we encounter in public places.

Are we, as the quotation suggests, contributors to this environment of anger and hostility? In my own life I confess to being both alarmed and ashamed of an experience I had last spring and summer that illustrates the pervasiveness of this hostile public climate. For almost thirty years my family and I have lived on the edge of a vest-pocket park, and until last year we enjoyed every minute of it. We love to watch toddlers learning to push, kick, and throw balls, college students throwing Frisbees, youngsters playing lacrosse, elderly couples walking hand in hand around the park.

Then last spring something happened. A group of teenagers began appearing about 2:30 every afternoon. The boys wore big baggy shorts, baseball caps turned backward, unkempt hair. The girls had long, straight hair, wore skirts down to their ankles, and boots. Sometimes they came in cars and sometimes on foot. Each day they sat in a circle and smoked—what, I am not sure. Sometimes they drank beer, sometimes soft drinks. When they left at about 6:00 P.M.—I assume to go home for dinner—the park looked like a disaster area. We and our neighbors took turns picking up after them. At first we began picking up trash before they left—naively hoping to shame them into helping. The Parks Department even moved a large green can over next to the big elm tree across from our house, hoping the kids would get the idea and pick up their garbage. The kids simply ignored us. Sometimes we had the feeling they were laughing at us.

Then they started coming at night. They showed up about 10:00 and stayed until 2:00 A.M., slamming car doors, breaking bottles, yelling back and forth at each other. Some mornings I picked up used condoms as well as beer bottles and smoked joints.

Our first reaction was shock. How could this be happening? Ours is a "nice," upper-middle-class, white neighborhood. These kids, we learned later, were also from "nice," upper-middle-class homes right in our neighborhood. We finally solved the problem, but it took perseverance and the skill of neighbors who were attorneys, bankers, corporate CEOs—sophisticated persons who have wide negotiating experience in this country and abroad.

My point in mentioning this incident is not to focus on what was done—spotlights installed in the park and police activity increased—or even on what happened to the kids, but rather on what happened to me. My greatest concern at the time was my own reaction as we dealt with the problem. First, I became afraid, genuinely scared to walk out in front of my house at night. How could this happen to someone who prided herself in being comfortable participating in inner-city ministry projects? Many of my neighbors expressed the same fear. We became part of that amorphous group we so often criticize—those who do not want to become involved for fear of what it will cost if they do. (We and some of our neighbors did experience some personal property vandalism during this time.)

Second, just looking at those kids made me furious, enraged. I wanted them punished. My feelings about those kids were much like their feelings about me—contemptuous, disdaining. They thought I was just some useless old lady who didn't know what it meant to have a good time. I thought they were irresponsible, lazy, spoiled brats.

But then there was the unforgettable statement the policeman made at one of our neighborhood meetings. "We've got this kind of kid all over the city now. Nobody wants them. Sure they have plenty of money and cars to drive around in all night. Nobody cares about them, but everybody hates them. Every neighborhood group like yours just wants us to get rid of them, send them someplace else—any place but here."

Most people feel that crime rates are rising, many would

say at an alarming rate. But crime experts tell us there is a disparity between the public's perception and the facts. According to statistics, the crime rate today is actually down. Perhaps the disparity is caused by fear over experiences like mine with the young people in the park. We are afraid because we are not treated with respect by those we meet publicly. Kindness and consideration give way to sullenness and contempt, making us uneasy.

Experiences such as mine remind us that we must approach abstract discussions of disagreements among Christians with a sense of genuine humility. It is much easier to talk about civility in dialogue concerning homosexuality, abortion, and euthanasia than to confront our own lifestyle fears and angers. Yet all our verbiage is hollow talk if we cannot be civil in our daily interactions. We must not be glib if we intend to join with others in the Christian community who resist the trend and say, "Enough! We will no longer tolerate disdain and contempt as the pervasive mood of social intercourse."

As we move from personal experiences to the generalized public arena, our concerns for civility in public discourse need to be seen in historic as well as theoretical perspective. The issues are broader, deeper, and more complex than the specific ideological conflicts that engulf the "hot" topics of abortion and homosexuality. These may be the most visible concerns, but they are only partial cause for the current polarization within society at large as well as in the Christian community.

ARE CHRISTIANITY AND TOLERANCE COMPATIBLE?

Can religion encourage tolerance or does it inevitably reinforce intolerance? Richard Mouw, in a piece titled "Religious Conviction and Public Civility," offers a succinct review of literature on the topic and offers his own analysis. Much of the material in this section comes from his work.[2]

Demonstrating the compatibility of Christianity and democracy is difficult. Christianity demands obedience to certain principles that believers hold to be eternal verities. Democracy is built on principles of flexibility and accommodation. Those who affirm democracy do so with confidence that a vigorous clash of opinions will, in the end, produce a satisfactory outcome, and that this is the best way for societies to make decisions about public policy. Christians who believe their faith's prescribed course of action is correct and must eventually prevail find it difficult to condone the high degree of flexibility that democracy requires.[3]

Martin Marty puts the question this way, "Can we reconcile the apparent conflict between conviction and civility [when in fact] the committed seem to lack civility and the civil often lack conviction?"[4] Many liberal Christians are filled with hope that convicted civility is attainable, but they know it will not be easy.

Civility has been defined as public politeness.[5] It demands that we display tact, niceness, moderation, refinement, good manners—all the stuff that modernization requires of people who want to be thought of as "civilized." These characteristics are indigenous to Judaism and Christianity. As Rabbi Arthur Hertzberg says, "The American experiment [is] something previously unknown and almost unthinkable of religions," namely, that "each sect is to remain the one true and revealed faith for itself and in private, but each must behave in the public arena as if its truth were as tentative as an aesthetic opinion or a scientific theory."[6] Christians who affirm democracy and believe in an ethic of tolerance must develop a strategy for coping with the present, imperfect state of affairs. Human decision making is not flawless. Some decisions made democratically result in tragic mistakes. Yet Christians who accept democracy find that, for all their flaws, democracies

51

build more humane communities than totalitarian states, even Christian ones. There is, however, a danger that an acceptance of all democratically arrived at decisions can result in a simplistic resignation to the imperfections of the world. Such acceptance easily becomes a type of Christian cynicism which should be avoided.[7]

RELIGION IN PUBLIC SPACE

Secular thinkers through time have been fond of blaming religious zeal for much of the polarization and intolerance in society as a whole. Those identified closely with communities of faith have been faced with the accusations that more wars have been fought in the name of religion than for any other reason. Rousseau, the eighteenth-century social philosopher, for example, insists in *The Social Contract* that "theological intolerance" must inevitably lead to "civil intolerance" since "one cannot live in peace with people one regards as damned."[8]

What is at stake here is our understanding of the relationship of religious conviction to public space. Rousseau wanted to establish conditions that would provide for a broad public arena devoted to the give-and-take of polite dialogue among mutually respectful citizens. He left the impression that only a secular society can provide a climate conducive to free-flowing public discourse. The intrusion of religious dogma, he felt, only inhibits such discourse.

On the other hand, Robert Bellah and his associates, who wrote *Habits of the Heart,* are convinced that it is precisely because public life has lost its grounding in the older religious and civic visions of life that the space devoted to civic dialogue has become cramped and crowded with individual interests. What is needed to correct the situation is the recovery and/or reinforcement of "communities of memory"—especially the churches and synagogues where "there are still operating among us . . . traditions that tell us about the nature of the world, about the nature of society, and about who we are as a people."[9] These are crucial to the health of a society.

This is a very different picture from the one painted by secularists. The inhibition of civil dialogue is due, not so much to religious dogma, as to the fragmenting of interests that occurs when a society loses its vision of what community and citizenship are all about.

SPIRITUAL BENEFITS OF CIVILITY

Contemporary sociologists express concern over the preoccupation with self that pervades American society, especially white, upper-middle-class society. Bellah's suggestion that we need to recover our religious understandings of the issues in public life is a way of effecting the much-needed opening up of our communal spaces for institutional transformation. Echoing the same theme, Richard Sennett, in his book *The Fall of Public Man*, suggests that in our obsession with intimate warmth in human affairs we have fostered what he calls an "ideology of intimacy [within which] social relationships of all kinds are considered real and believable the closer they approach the inner psychological concerns of each person."[10] This process transmutes political categories into psychological categories. Such psychologizing of all human interaction also destroys the bonds of association and mutual commitment that exist between people who are not joined by ties of family or intimate association. As a society we may be in danger of losing our sense of the value of "the bond of the crowd, of a 'people,' or a polity."[11]

Think back now to the incident in the park I described earlier. The high school students, and unfortunately the neighbors to a lesser degree, illustrate the phenomenon. The kids were there with their friends; they felt no bond to "the public," to a shared communal life in which all members of the corpus can mutually experience the public space. Each intimate group, neighbors and youngsters, saw the situation as "us or them." Each group asked, in effect, "How does *our* intimate group want to use the resource?" We had lost the connections between one intimate group and another.

A SIGN OF HOPE

Lest we become too discouraged, a description of a second incident in that same park is in order. In this second situation a community group did recover a particularized religious understanding that opened up a public space.

This spring, on Good Friday, a group of clergy decided to experiment with an ecumenical Stations of the Cross service in the park. Sponsors were Protestant and Catholic churches located within a few blocks of the park. The clergyperson who described the plan observed that the planners had no idea whether it would work but decided to risk the effort. "I'll be happy if five people show up." By my count about two hundred persons came for all or part of the time—it was difficult to count accurately as outsiders kept joining in. The clergy were robed, and there was a crucifer who carried the cross from one spot in the park to another. At each stop, one of the Good Friday readings was followed by a few sentences of comment and prayer. The group then moved on while singing, "Jesus Remember Me," led by choir members from the churches.

Once we stopped beside a homeless man who was asleep when we arrived, but he sat up and listened intently. He prayed with us. At another spot we met some teenagers with pierced body parts. They too joined us for a while. People in cars and those walking in the park stopped to listen or watch. Nobody was disrespectful. Later a number of neighbors who are not church members asked if this could happen every year, "It was such a nice thing to do."

In the language of the sociology of religion, religious ceremonies such as this create social solidarity. They remind society at large of a universal obligation of love and concern for others that can be generalized beyond the specificity of the religious event experienced.

An event such as this one gives Christians the opportunity to do something for the public realm. That is good, but an equal good comes back to the Christian community in what the public realm can teach them about their own spiritual identity. If we believe that God loves all persons then we must become involved in the whole world, in the public spaces. Mouw suggests that we must learn to go into the world with a "soft public self"—not the softness of intimacy, but a gentleness of spirit and behavior with which we can embrace others who are different. Experiences such as this one teach us something of how we can remain faithful to our belief in a peaceful society and our trust of all persons as children of God, without being unduly naïve and stupid about the reality of situations in which meanness and danger exist.

Recently I used this illustration as part of a lecture given to a group of clergy from across the country who were attending a continuing education event. Several of them were quick to point out that a religious ceremony such as this one, performed on public property, might well be disallowed by certain city or state ordinances. The observation is valid. Our city, like many throughout the country, has a huge display of Christmas lights that graces the City and County Building each year. Our display depicts Santa Claus with lots of elves and reindeer, but no Mary, no Joseph, no manger, and no baby. Yet in the same city we are experiencing a campaign to keep homeless persons displaying signs saying, "Will work for food," off busy street corners. Friends in the legal profession tell me that the campaign will not prevail. The First Amendment protects the right of all persons to free speech. Perhaps the Good Friday walk across public property was illegal. However, if such small neighborhood events are illegal, Christians may, on occasions such as this, need to risk civil disobedience.

LACK OF CIVILITY WITHIN THE CHRISTIAN COMMUNITY

Unfortunately, Christians don't always work together well, and there is a serious lack of civility between Christian groups. Barnett Pearce and his colleagues describe the interaction between the new Christian right and secular humanists as acrimonious, and have analyzed its patterns.[12] The blurring of the lines between secular humanists and liberal Christians led me to assume the authors were contrasting the religious right with the religious left as well as with secular humanists. Obviously there are significant differences in the theology that undergirds liberal Christians and secular humanists. However, Pearce's typology can help us analyze the communication difficulties between liberal and conservative Christians.

This group of authors seems rather pessimistic about the possibility of productive dialogue between these groups. However, they conclude their analysis with an admonition that attempts at dialogue must be continued if our society is to remain whole. Senator Edward Kennedy, a Roman Catholic, is a prime example of a secular humanist who has tried to engage the right in civil dialogue. The authors caution that we must work to avoid the common historic conclusion of ideologic battles of this nature because too often one side is silenced and repressed. As Christians we can afford neither to be repressed nor to repress.

HISTORY OF THE INTERACTION[13]

In the 1960s proponents of all institutionalized religion were on the defensive, as were those who supported traditional higher education, our government's intervention in Vietnam, and traditional rules for sexual conduct. By the late 1970s conservative Christians found themselves spurned by the cultural mainstream, which by then included secular humanists along with liberal Christians and Jews. Some conservatives welcomed the role of outside critic. Others felt caught between "spiritual" and "political" obligations. In the mid-1970s Jerry Falwell was still preaching against involvement in political and worldly things. Christianity was about personal salvation, not political reform.

But in 1979 Falwell established the Moral Majority, and conservative Christians entered a new period of interaction with the rest of society. At first the religious right was considered ineffectual and not worth worrying about in public discourse. That judgment of the movement came to an abrupt end, however, with the elections of 1980 and 1982. The Christian right successfully negotiated itself into a position of political power, with access to the White House and to Congress. It began setting the agenda: abortion, homosexuality, feminism, secular education, and pornography were their issues.

From that point on, other Americans began to take the religious right seriously, recognizing the necessity of trying to establish some kind of dialogue. One opportunity came about when Edward Kennedy mistakenly received a mailing from the Moral Majority in which he was urged to send money to combat "ultraliberals such as Ted Kennedy." The embarrassment caused by the incident led to an invitation for Kennedy to speak at Liberty Baptist College in 1983. From then on he and Falwell shared the platform on numerous occasions, and he appeared jointly with Falwell at the National Religious Broadcasters convention in 1985. Columnist Cal Thomas referred to them as the traveling "Odd Couple."

Once taken seriously, the new Christian right provoked surprisingly intemperate responses from the mainstream of American society. For example, the president of Yale called their agenda "dangerous, malicious nonsense." The American Civil Liberties Union took out a full page ad in the *New York Times* suggesting that "if the Moral Majority has its way you had better start praying."[14] The new Christian right responded to the criticism by making its own pronouncement. For example, one of their advertisements in the *New York Times* suggested that the "Moral Majority, Inc. is made up of millions of Americans . . . who are deeply concerned about the moral decline of our nation, and who are sick and tired of the way many amoral and secular humanists and liberals are destroying the traditional family and moral values on which our nation was built."[15]

It is important to note, that most of the criticism of the right was made by individuals. However the responses were always phrased as corporate responses: "We must not stand by while millions of unborn babies are killed" or "We must halt the invasion of our cities by perverts who bring the plague of AIDS." This intentionally constructed public persona allows one individual to speak with a voice greater than his own. Too often this technique convinces the public at large that the proponent of the point of view has a large following. That may not be the case. The Moral Majority never represented a majority of American citizens, or even a majority of Christians.

A lot of the rhetoric implies that the conflict is between groups. However, identifying who is in the groups is not as easy as many assume. Pearce and the other sociologists who wrote about this earlier period suggest that for purposes of analysis it is best to view new Christian right organizations as the voice of a cultural perspective rather than as traditional organizations. Often a charismatic leader is involved—Jerry Falwell, for example, or Ralph Reed, or James Dobson.

There is substantial evidence that the leader is often

much more extreme in his conservatism than are most of the members of the culture he purports to represent. This disparity between leader and followers deserves careful attention from liberals who may become unduly alarmed over the influence of the religious right. James Davison Hunter[16] pointed out the disparity when reporting results of a 1980s research study with young evangelicals. He found that evangelical college students and seminarians were "solidly tolerant" on a civil liberties index. When asked about approval of the Moral Majority agenda, 1 percent of the students at public universities approved, 2 percent of the students at evangelical universities, and 5 percent of the evangelical seminarians.

ANALYSIS OF INTERACTION BETWEEN LEFT AND RIGHT

Pearce and his colleagues developed a set of characteristics to describe dialogue between conservatives and liberals. For example, discourse *within* each group is richer than discourse *between* groups. Each side, when speaking to itself, locates itself in a sociohistoric context and presents pure motives and methods. When the sides come together, each side feels threatened by the other, and each perceives the other side as differing in position on political issues. However anyone interested in understanding the depth of the disagreement must take careful notice of the way in which each side builds its arguments. Entirely different approaches are used. The two groups disagree fundamentally on the *ways* in which people should come to decisions about issues. Conservatives base their arguments on a set of absolute biblical principles that should regulate human behavior. Liberals base their arguments on more flexible principles of conduct, and place emphasis on the Christian virtues of kindness, hospitality, and mercy. It is this difference in approach to decision making that causes dialogue to fall apart when the sides come together for conversation. Liberals see conservatives as foolish; conservatives see liberals as unthinking. When the sides start from differing assumptions and use data differently, they do not "engage" each other when they try to interact. This lack of engagement is the element that causes the analysts to be pessimistic about productive dialogue.

If this analysis of the interaction is correct, it is not accurate or helpful to view the conflicts as merely disagreement on issues. For liberals, subordinating oneself to dogma requires precisely the mind-set they believe all Christians should overcome. Being urged to adopt such a stance appears frightful. For members of the new Christian right, entrusting oneself to the conclusions of human reason seems hazardous, leaving one in danger of adopting an erroneous lifestyle. More important, perhaps, trusting human reason leaves one with no basis for certainty in moral questions, and without certainty persons find themselves helpless and adrift.

"The issue is not really *what* to think but *how;* not so much what specific *acts* are right or wrong but how *morality* is to be determined."[17] To illustrate the differences between worldview and specific acts, the authors remind us that the National Organization for Women and the Moral Majority coalesced to fight pornography. However, their cooperation was *not* a sign of "agreement."[18]

POSITIVE SUGGESTIONS, HOPEFUL SIGNS

Given the pessimism of the preceding analysis, we might ask, Is the situation hopeless? Can Christians with different perspectives ever disagree in love? We can find hope by thinking of the interactions in which each of us is involved. Most of us have family members, childhood or college friends, professional colleagues and/or fellow church members who hold strong convictions on both sides of these religious arguments. In some situations these ideological differences are allowed to rip apart the fabric of love and concern that normally binds together persons in close association with one another. In other relationships the same persons seem able to transcend the differences. Some characteristics or principles seem to be followed quite consistently by those who can transcend deep differences, who can disagree in love. Here are some of them, illustrated by experiences that have happened for me when the principles were followed.

1. *Refrain from absolutist judgments. Almost no person or group is altogether evil or altogether saintly.*

We once had a next-door neighbor named Ed who was a dyed-in-the-wool conservative. He was against affirmative action, the women's movement, and anything that went with it, including abortion rights and government-subsidized child care for working mothers. He was against almost everything else our family affirmed. And worst of all he sometimes quoted the Bible!

During the early years of our relationship we felt nothing but contempt for him and spoke to him as infrequently as possible. Privately we judged him to be a bigoted, racist, sexist pig. He did not care for us either and frequently referred to me as the neighborhood's bleeding heart. However, his little girl, Laura, was our three-year-old son's favorite playmate, so we, the parents, tolerated one another for the sake of the children.

One winter Laura contracted such a serious infection that she was hospitalized. When visiting Laura in her two-bed room, I came upon Ed with his back to the door. At first he was unaware of anyone watching him. He was standing beside the very black child in the other bed. She must have been in an accident because both of her arms were in splints, so she could not feed herself. Ed was leaning over the bed, spoon in hand, saying, "Now one more bite and you can have the ice cream."

61

Finally, sensing my presence he turned around, gave me a sheepish look and said, "Her mother is at work, the nurses are too busy to feed her right now. So what was I to do?"

We never mentioned the incident again, but he quit calling me the neighborhood's bleeding heart, and we began thinking of him more kindly. We never became fast friends, but on the other hand we were able to cooperate on a number of worthwhile neighborhood projects, such as building a playground.

2. Beware of your own dogmatism. Remember it is possible to overstate one's position when passions run high in an ideological conflict.

As a member of my denomination's study committee on homosexuality I have been outspoken in my insistence on the acceptance of gay and lesbian persons in all phases of church life, including ordination. Most of the negative mail that crossed my desk came from persons who seemed quite irrational in their anger. However, one letter gave me pause.

The writer told me that my father had been her doctor, so she knew where I grew up. Didn't I remember, she asked, what it was like living in a small community, where relatives and friends—including some of mine—were very prejudiced and used words like "nigger," "kike," or "queer"? Did I really think that any homosexual minister, especially one with a live-in partner, appointed to any small church in those areas would ever be accepted?

It took a long time to construct an answer. In the end my response acknowledged the reality of some of her remarks. She deserved an apology if my comments seemed to overgeneralize my affirmation of open pastoral appointments. Of course not every pastor is suited to every local church. My letter ended with a request to her not to overgeneralize about my rural relatives and their friends. When it comes to fair treatment of persons, my family has as much integrity as any other even if they have some prejudices.

3. Try to find out why *the person or persons holding a different ideological position feel as they do. Understanding keeps one from feeling angry with or superior to persons with whom you disagree.*

A member of my church once called and asked me to meet with her in order to discuss her concern over my public advocacy of legislation that provides legal access to abortion. When we met she told me that some years ago she, too, had been an advocate for abortion rights, but something happened that changed her mind. After her daughter was old enough to start grade school, she returned to college and pursued a law degree. Right at a critical time in her studies, however, she became pregnant. One child was more than enough for her to care for right then; having another child was too inconvenient. So she had an abortion. Not long after this her little girl was struck by lightning in a freak accident on the school yard. The child died. The woman came from a very conservative religious background and is convinced that the accident was not an accident at all but rather a punishment from God for her sin of not carrying the second child to term.

As the tears streamed down her face, I thought about my own healthy children. It was not possible for me to utter the rational words my intellect suggested as a response: "What you believe is wrong. Your daughter's death was an accident. God does not punish that way. In your grief you have gotten all mixed up. There is no reason for you to torture yourself. Your pain has nothing to do with abortion rights. My advice is that you should see a good mental health professional and get your thinking straightened out."

Another voice inside me said, *Sally, who do you think you are? God? What right have you to judge her? Her reality is as true for her as yours is for you.* So I simply took her hand and told her I was sorry that my actions troubled her so. It did not change my convictions, but it did change my attitude toward some who disagree with me about abortion.

When I was a child my mother told me that being a Christian was not going to be easy. She was correct. It is not easy to listen when you are angry or to be kind when

63

you are misunderstood or ignored. But Jesus commanded us to treat others as we would have them treat us. It takes hard work to develop the sensitivity that will enable us to understand each other's pain as well as each other's joy. As part of the human family, each of us must care for all the members, each and every one. As Christians we live in the hope that through God's grace we will know how.

SUMMARY

In this chapter we have asked questions about the possibility of building a climate of understanding between Christians on the religious right and those on the religious left. First we asked whether Christianity and tolerance are compatible, particularly during this bitter conflict about lifestyle issues such as abortion and homosexuality. Compatibility is difficult to demonstrate when some Christians believe the Bible offers a firm, specific code of behavior and other Christians believe the Bible offers guidelines within which democratic dialogue guided by kindness and compassion can produce a flexible set of rules for behavior.

Next we questioned the relationship of religion and the current lack of civility of interaction within public space. Perhaps the lack of civility is caused by our loss of grounding in an older, religious vision of public dialogue. We may need to reclaim our "communities of memory" if Americans are to become less concerned with self and less contemptuous of one another.

When we analyzed the patterns of interaction between Christians who disagree fiercely with one another over lifestyle issues, we learned that much of the rhetoric from the religious right comes from leaders who create a public persona that allows an individual to speak with a voice greater than his own. Often the views of leaders are more extreme than those of their constituency.

A major obstacle to dialogue between the sides is the disparity between their understandings about the ways in which persons should come to decisions about issues. Conservatives base their arguments on a set of absolute biblical principles that should regulate human behavior. Liberals base their arguments on more flexible principles of conduct and place emphasis on the Christian virtues of kindness, hospitality, and mercy. It is this difference in approach rather than convictions about the specific issues themselves that causes dialogue to break down.

Finally we offered suggestions for improved relationships between persons on opposing sides. Christians are called to refrain from absolutistic judgments, to beware of their own dogmatism—none of us fully comprehend God's will—and to listen compassionately to the stories of other persons with whom they do not agree.

In the next chapter we will tackle a different conflict: the escalating racial tension in America. Our questions focus primarily on the roles white persons play in intensifying the conflict.

FOR REFLECTION

1. Arthur Hertzberg implies that religious freedom works well only if each group adopts one attitude in private and a different attitude in public. In private, each group can treat its beliefs as the one true and revealed faith. But in public every group must act as if all religious beliefs are tentative—more like scientific theories.

Is this the way religious freedom works in your denomination? How do the liberal and conservative groups treat each other?

2. Richard Sennett suggests that one reason our society has lost its cohesion is that we have fostered an ideology of intimacy, meaning that we only feel responsible for the care of persons in our immediate circle of family and friends. Do you agree or disagree?

3. How do you deal with those whose opinions differ strongly from yours? Do you follow the social rule, "Never discuss religion or politics"? How do you decide when to debate and when to keep quiet?

NOTES

1. George Mitrovich and Jim Wallis, "The Age of Rudeness: Restore Civility to Political Discourse," *The Denver Post,* April 28, 1996, p. E4.

2. Richard J. Mouw, "Religious Conviction and Public Civility," chapter 7 in *Ethics, Religion and the Good Society: New Directions in a Pluralistic World,* ed. Joseph Runzo (Louisville: Westminster/John Knox Press, 1992), pp. 95-109.

3. This paragraph summarizes the arguments advanced by Donald Atwell Zoll, *Twentieth Century Political Philosophy* (Englewood Cliffs, N.J.: Prentice Hall, 1974), p. 94, as quoted by Mouw, "Religious Conviction and Public Civility," p. 95.

4. Martin Marty, *By Way of Response* (Nashville: Abingdon Press, 1981), p. 81, as quoted in Mouw, "Religious Conviction and Public Civility," p. 96.

5. John Murray Cuddihy, *The Ordeal of Civility: Freud, Marx, Levi-Strauss, and the Jewish Struggle with Modernity* (New York: Basic Books, 1974), p. 235, as quoted in Mouw, p. 96.

6. Quoted by Cuddihy, *The Ordeal of Civility,* as cited in Mouw, "Religious Conviction and Public Civility," p. 96.

7. Glenn Tinder, quoted by Cuddihy, *No Offense: Civil Religion and Protestantism* (New York: Seabury Press, 1978), p. 211, as cited in Mouw, "Religious Conviction and Public Civility," p. 106.

8. Jean Jacques Rousseau, *The Social Contract,* trans. by Willmoore Kendall (Chicago: Henry Regnery, 1954), p. 160, as quoted in Mouw, "Conviction and Public Civility," p. 97.

9. Robert Bellah, et al., *Habits of the Heart* (New York: Harper & Row, 1986).

10. Richard Sennett, *The Fall of Public Man: On the Social Psychology of Capitalism* (New York: Vintage Books, 1978), p. 259, as quoted in Mouw, "Religious Conviction and Public Civility," p. 99.

11. Ibid.

12. W. Barnett Pearce, Stephen W. Littlejohn, and Alison Alexander, "Quest for Civility: Patterns of Interaction Between the New Christian Right and Secular Humanists," in *Secularization and Fundamentalism Reconsidered: Religion and the Political Order,* vol. III, edited by Jeffrey Hadden and Anson Shupe (New York: Paragon House, 1989), pp. 152-77. This book is dedicated to Barbara Hargrove, my friend and Iliff colleague. Her untimely death has diminished the number of fine Christian scholars working in the area of religion and sociology.

13. Most of the material in this section paraphrases material found in Pearce, et al., "Quest for Civility."

14. Pearce, "Quest for Civility," p. 156.

15. Ibid.

16. James Davison Hunter, "Religion and Political Civility: The Coming Generation of American Evangelicals," *Journal for the Scientific Study of Religion,* 1984 (23, 4): 364-80.

17. Pearce, et al., "Quest for Civility," p. 174.

18. Ibid.

CHAPTER THREE

White Christians As Recovering Racists

INTRODUCTION

The deterioration of family values is a primary concern for many Christians, particularly conservative ones. The escalation of racial tension is a primary concern for others, mostly liberal ones. It can be argued that the problems are closely related. Conservatives feel we must strengthen family values in order to preserve our way of life, which is deteriorating in a social climate of violence and fear. Liberals feel we must address fear and misunderstanding based on race if we are to build a safer, friendlier America. Ideally both problems can be worked on simultaneously by Christians of all ideological perspectives. Scripture commands us to make love of neighbor one of our highest priorities.

In today's America our neighbors are more likely to be yellow, black, white, red, and brown than at any other time in our history.[1] Yet it seems obvious that the leadership and membership in powerful Protestant denominations are still predominately white. Apparently few persons of color find these institutions safe, hospitable places in which to receive spiritual nurture. Those persons of color who do hold leadership positions, as well as most of those who attend predominately white churches, are middle to upper middle class and tend to conform to white, middle-class patterns of dress, speech, and lifestyle.

This chapter is meant for all well-meaning, white Christians who belong to those churches and sincerely believe they are kind and prejudice-free, not racist. I am not writing to persuade those who belong to white supremacist groups that they are bigoted. My argument is that most white Christians fail to understand how racist they are, whether they mean to or not. Our intentions are good, but we do not understand how our messages are received—and we all know where the road paved with good intentions leads!

The analysis offered here is predicated on the assumption that renewal of the church must include progress toward the eradication of white racism. The resolution of racial conflict depends more on alterations in the behavior of white people than on alterations in the behavior of nonwhite people. This is not to deny the existence of nonwhite prejudice. It exists, and it too is a problem. However, it is not the focus of the chapter. We who are white need to put our own house in order before we worry about nonwhite prejudice. Here I want to describe white racism within some specific contexts, discuss its roots, and suggest some possible steps toward resolution.

Another exclusion needs to be understood. Tension between white people and poor people who are often assumed to be people of color is not the focus of the chapter. Economic inequality is of tremendous importance. Too often, however, white people tend to believe that discussions about solving "the race problem" are by definition discussions of raising poor people out of poverty. That implies that white people must do more for persons of color. This chapter intentionally uncouples race and poverty in order to show that white racism exists even when economic deprivation is not an issue.

WHOSE PROBLEM IS IT?

When George Tinker says that all white people in the United States are racist, but some of us are recovering racists, white people are usually shocked and hurt.[2] It is particularly painful for persons who call themselves Christians to hear this Native American seminary professor accuse them of racism. Many react defensively. How dare he make such an accusation! Yet there is more truth to his indictment than most of us care to admit.

Within the last few years white Christians have been confronted with evidence that the civil rights movement of the 1960s did not make Dr. Martin Luther King's dream come true. The videotaped incident of white policemen beating Rodney King in the early 1990s, so difficult to watch, demonstrated that. We hoped and prayed that it was an unusual incident. Later evidence, however, about police brutality did little to confirm this hope, particularly when the officers were found not guilty in a court of law. We were further disturbed when Jim Wallis, a respected religious leader, linked the verdict in the Rodney King case to advertisements used in George Bush's campaign for presidential reelection. The advertisement played on fears that Governor Michael Dukakis was too soft on crime to be president. The proof was a graphic portrayal of Willie Horton, a black man who committed murder and was sent to prison but then paroled. He committed another violent crime while on parole. "When presidents use racial fears and stereotypes to get elected, white jurors feel justified in using them, too."[3]

Another perturbing, recent event was the O. J. Simpson trial. Its drama gripped the nation for weeks. White people seemed stunned at the verdict and even more astonished at the depth of emotion with which many blacks defended the jury that acquitted Simpson. Apparently most of us who are white had no idea that nonwhite persons are so distrustful of the legal system in this country, so sure that persons of color will be treated unfairly. We had hardly recovered from the Simpson trial when the newspapers became full of stories about the number of black churches recently burned to the ground. According to Dr. Joan Campbell, head of the National Council of Churches, "more than 60 African-American and multiracial churches were burned between January 1, 1995 and June 30, 1996, more than in the previous five years combined . . . black churches are being burned in proportion to their number at four times the rate of white churches."[4]

These figures, supported with independent studies by the U.S. Justice Department, are so disturbing that some white Christians seek to deny them. For example, Diane Knippers, head of the Institute for Religion and Democracy, a conservative think tank, has said, "The NCC has exaggerated the church burning phenomenon so as . . . to smear conservatives, especially conservative Christians, as racists."[5] Probably many liberal Christians as well as conservative ones are disconcerted by the stories and want to deny what they imply about the racism of all whites, including Christians.

White surprise and confusion stem, in part, from some mistaken assumptions. One is that the civil rights movement of the 1960s cured the discriminatory practices that fueled our racial ills. Another is that affirmative action has unjustly favored nonwhite persons. Anger is intense over the loss of job opportunities presumably caused by affirmative action. White males are particularly angry. Fear of affirmative action is intensified, if not caused by, concern over the changing nature of the job market and job insecurity among middle-class working people. A growing group of white persons believe that if nonwhite persons are still having problems this long after the civil rights movement, it must be their fault. In the first year of Jimmy Carter's administration, Benjamin Hooks told a convention of

Urban League delegates that "nearly 80 percent of the white people in America feel that enough has been done for black people."[6] Such sentiment is increasingly popular. It fuels the erosion of affirmative action laws and the dissolution of the federal welfare program begun in Franklin Roosevelt's administration.

However, black reaction to the Simpson verdict reminds white people that people of color are angry too. They are enraged by the preferential treatment they believe white persons receive in every dimension of public life. They find differences of treatment before the law, in schools, in places of business, and even in the church. We who are white wonder how this newly discovered rage may be used against us. Persons of color worry about how white rage will be used against them. With so little mutual trust we all live in a state of increasing racial isolation and fear.

WHAT WORKED BEFORE IS NOT WORKING NOW

White persons who take church life seriously feel an obligation to try to relieve these racial tensions. Yet we are perplexed, not knowing how to proceed in order to accomplish the task. Techniques we used to relieve racial tension in the past do not work well anymore. Few people even remember the satisfaction white and nonwhite persons felt with the progress made in the 1960s. Those who marched with Dr. Martin Luther King, Jr., who sat-in at lunch counters or who registered voters, felt good about their accomplishments. They were confident that what they did made a difference. We yearn for the good old days when everybody seemed to know what it meant to "do the right thing."[7] Now we all understand Spike Lee's fine film by that title, in which an interracial group of persons tear their community apart almost by accident. Nobody seems to know what it means anymore to "do the right thing."

Older persons who worked in the civil rights movement of the 1960s still take pride in much of the legislation it produced. Today public facilities are, by law, open to persons regardless of race, religion, or national origin. Some establishments may seem friendlier than others, but all are legally open to persons of color. Few Americans would deny that such rules are moral as well as just. This was progress. However, it was not the end of racism. Something went wrong, and many of us harbor a fear that the relationships among persons of different races are more fraught with rage and anger than ever before. Perhaps most troublesome of all are the indications that many young people are disillusioned. They are not only disenchanted with the programs old-time liberals supported, but are quite despondent over the seeming impossibility of making things any better.

A WASP PERSPECTIVE

Before we can discuss developing new patterns of interaction between persons of different races we must describe the background out of which our white anger and current tensions grow.

Most older church members who are white, Anglo-Saxon Protestants (WASPs) grew up in small-town America before the civil rights movement. The midwestern and western communities in which many lived were populated by a high majority of persons from backgrounds just like theirs. As in southern communities, the persons of color who lived in small-town America were primarily servants or employed in other menial jobs. Seldom, if ever, did WASPs encounter work colleagues or social friends who were different from themselves. (Ironically this arrangement seems as prevalent today. Fear of crime, distress over urban noise and pollution and a desire for privacy are driving increasing numbers of affluent white people into planned suburban communities, high-rise apartments, condominium complexes with guards and gates, or resort communities. They too see persons of color primarily as servants.)

When one lives in a homogeneous community it is easy to forget that there is a discrimination problem. For example, during the 1930s in my hometown our racial mix consisted of three Jewish families and a few African American families who lived north of the tracks. Of course we had Christmas and Easter programs in the white schools. Nobody asked how that might affect the Jewish children.

All the Negro children went to the "colored" school on their side of the tracks until they were of high school age. Since there were so few of them, the town could not afford a separate high school, so they were allowed to come to "our" school. They seemed to understand they were to "stay in their place." That meant being invisible except on the football field, and we certainly welcomed them there. They did not speak in class or participate in extracurricular activities other than sports.

"Colored" people knew they could not eat in a restaurant, use a public bathroom, clerk in a store, or buy things in most stores. Even trying on clothes was forbidden. Of course they went to their own churches. Some white people approved of the arrangement; some simply did not think about it much one way or the other; some did not even realize it was true. Our white ignorance came to mind recently when one of the Negro graduates of our high school was asked to return as an honoree in the high school Hall of Fame. Dr. Virginia Hill Ricard, a college professor and international vice president of Girl Scouts and Girl Guides, accepted the honor.

Some members of our graduating class had gone to college with Ginny and had kept in contact with her over the years. So several of us returned to our home community for the occasion. In her speech Dr. Ricard reminded the audience that, though she was a good student with ambitions to succeed, her mother often told her, "You're just a poor colored girl, and don't you forget it." Many of us had not understood that when we were growing up.

Looking back on those times, we remembered that Ginny never went with us to the corner drugstore after school because, as she told us, she always had to get right home to help her mother. It never occurred to most of us that she did not come because the proprietor would not let her come into the drugstore and sit at the counter with us.

My parents were among the liberal whites who objected to the discriminatory laws and tried to make changes. For example, some of my childhood birthday parties were held at the Trailways bus station because the bus company allowed Negroes to eat there and go to the bathroom. Mother felt we should support that openness.

Black people frequently came to my parents for help with everything from access to medical care to assistance in persuading the high school principal it would be all right to let the colored students come to the junior-senior prom. After a rather heated discussion, it was finally decided that they could come if the Negro boys promised not to dance with the white girls.

The role that caring white people like my mother played was referred to in the black community as the role of "nice white lady." In those days most Negroes were grateful for nice white folks who could be counted on to intervene on their behalf. When one has no power in a social system, any avenue to power is helpful. We who were white understood that we were needed and appreciated. Our parents and church school teachers taught us to remember how fortunate we were and how important it was for us to help others. It was our version of the white man's burden. The word *patronizing* was never used to describe us.

74

NOSTALGIA FOR THE OLD RULES

Thoughts about that era came back to me during the 1996 Republican convention when Robert Dole gave his acceptance speech for the party's presidential nomination. He described growing up in Russell, Kansas, as the American dream we want to recapture as we enter a new century. I grew up in a town just a few miles east of Russell. Our family farm is just beyond Russell to the west. Bob Dole's memories and mine are both similar and different. He remembers it as a place of safety and freedom. It was that kind of place, at least for persons who understood the rules and played by them. However, a few miles west of Russell and my family's homestead is a town named Nicodemus. After the War between the States some freed slaves founded this community, bought the surrounding land, and farmed. In all the summers I spent on our farm as a child we had no contact with the citizens of Nicodemus. The commonly understood but seldom-spoken rules of the region set the boundaries. It was unsafe for anyone who lived in Nicodemus to be caught outside their own community after dark. Even in the daytime they stayed close to home.

Our family, like Mr. Dole's, arrived poor and prospered. Much of their success came through hard work. However, the initial economic opportunity that the Kansas territory offered to white homesteaders like my forebears was the farm- and ranch land they were given about a hundred years ago by the U.S. government. Our family is proud that the title to the homestead has never changed hands. We seldom remember that the land was taken from the Native American tribes who had lived there for generations. Russell and Salina may have exemplified the American dream for white Americans like Bob Dole and me. I do not know what memories are aroused in the minds of adults who grew up in Nicodemus when they recall their childhoods. However, I am reasonably sure their memories are different from Bob Dole's or mine. They have their own interpretation of the American dream.

The Midwest is not the only part of America that white Christians may remember more fondly than some other persons do. Representative Susan Molinari gave the keynote address at Mr. Dole's nominating convention and told about her East Coast, urban family's success with the American dream. She spoke of a grandfather who came to this country and opened a barbershop in Queens. She used his red, white, and blue barber pole as a symbol of the American dream. On hearing her remark, a Jewish friend of mine was reminded of his experiences with barbers while growing up in Queens. He found it necessary to cross over to Manhattan and go up to 125th Street for his haircuts. Only in Harlem would they cut "kinky" hair like his.

The point is not to denigrate Kansas farmers or New York shopkeepers. Most pioneers in all parts of the country were hardworking people looking for a better life to share with their families. Many succeeded through perseverance and sacrifice. However, those of us who reaped the benefits of that hard work need to temper our remembrances with an understanding of how much our success cost others.

When honest and caring white persons of integrity such as Robert Dole and Susan Molinari express nostalgia for American society of the past and also affirm racial inclusiveness they send the kind of message that caused George Tinker to say whites are recovering racists. The tendency of whites to romanticize the past is not confined to persons in one political party. It permeates all of society.

BAD NEWS AS WELL AS GOOD ABOUT PROGRESS IN CIVIL RIGHTS

For whites the bad news about progress made in the civil rights movement is that it produced some unintended consequences. As persons of color gained some power of their own, they became less willing to be grateful for assistance from white people. They were no longer as gracious to "nice" white people as they had been in the past. Their altered attitudes and behavior have left many well-meaning white people fearful and uncertain about how they are supposed to treat persons of other races. When the rules of discrimination were rigid and clear, at least everyone knew what role she or he was to play. We yearn for those days when there was less confrontation and conflict. We felt more confident then about what to say and how to behave.

Unfortunately, the graciousness of those days was tainted with the reality of white domination. We mistakenly believed that coupling repression with kindness made life good for persons of color as well as for us. Few Christians understood the inadequacy of our behavior. We were taught to be charitable to the poor and tolerant of differences. However, charity too often meant giving what you no longer needed yourselves. Tolerance meant listening politely when persons of color complained about being ignored. It did not require that one feel any real pressure to accept or incorporate the others' point of view into the decision-making process. These relationships across racial lines were not reciprocal. We were generous; they were grateful. We had something to offer; they had something to learn. Our generosity was an offer to teach persons of color how to be like us. We assumed they should accept white ways of doing business and raising families as well as dressing, eating, and talking. In those days we felt a great sense of security following our rules. We dislike the confrontational attitude with which many persons of color treat us today. We are angry when they fail to perform at the level we expect. We are furious when they then assume, correctly, that they can get by with shoddy performance because we are afraid to reprimand them and risk being called racist.

SUBTLE FORMS OF RACISM

As overt forms of discrimination diminish, other forms of racism continue to plague the lives of persons of color. These more subtle forms of racism often go undetected by white persons, even those with the best intentions. A significant experience in my own ongoing journey toward understanding racism occurred during the 1980s. At that time much of my professional energy was consumed by various research projects in the psychiatry department of a teaching hospital. My primary research colleague was Ruth L. Fuller, whom I mentioned earlier.[8] Our research required that we work closely together and depend on each other. The experience deepened my understanding of the insidious effects of white racism on her professional life and on our project.[9]

It also led to unsettling conclusions about myself and my well-meaning white colleagues. Most of us who are white acknowledge that some discrimination still exists, and we find it morally repugnant. What we may not accept as readily is a belief that discrimination exists within our own decision making. The problem is so subtle and so ingrained that it must be described in context if it is to be made credible. George Tinker explains it this way:

> Racism, that is, the exercise of White privilege, is an addiction. If it is an addictive pattern of behavior . . . the problem lies in the structures of the addictive process itself. Not only is White privilege deeply rooted in the psyche, rooted in ways that are often unnoticeable to the addict (that is, every White American), but the structure of society itself continues to reward, quite often very subtly, but definitely, whiteness and those who play by the rules that ensure the continuation of White privilege.[10]

What follows is an example of white privilege at work. Its context was a teaching hospital. The same conditions,

78

however, probably exist in most other bureaucratic organizations, including departments of government, school districts, business corporations, or religious denominations.

SUBTLE RACISM—AN EXAMPLE

The investigation that Dr. Fuller and I undertook dealt with the effects of newborn skin color and changes in skin color on maternal bonding. Dr. Fuller's belief that the subject was worthy of investigation grew out of her own life experience with childbirth. Her first child was born with lovely mahogany-colored skin. To her amazement and chagrin, however, her second child looked lily white at birth. Nothing in her medical training explained the disaster. She needed help to understand, but all of the staff were white and she was reluctant to discuss the problem with them.

Only when she called a beloved aunt did she discover that many African American babies are born quite white. However, there are ways to tell what color the child will be "when the color does come in." Her aunt suggested that she look at the base of his fingernails and along the edge of his ear. If there was a dark line in those places, that was the color he would be in about a month. With relief, Ruth discovered he did have such lines. However, she was struck with the realization that there was nothing in her medical curriculum about this phenomenon, which can cause so much anxiety for minority patients. Now, as a teaching faculty member in a medical school, she was interested in determining how many present-day healthcare staff members are trained to know what impact infant skin color can have on black mothers. Do we still allow young, black mothers to worry in silence if they do not have another black person to teach them what her aunt taught her?

Our first encounter with the subtle effects of institutional racism on our work came when we inquired about potential funding sources. Each of us made inquiry and each of us was given information about sources that traditionally fund infant research. However, when I, the white member of the team, asked about sources, the university officer with whom we worked ended our conversation with a seemingly casual remark, "It seems like a funny project. I don't know for sure who would be interested in little black babies." Not until Dr. Fuller made me aware did the importance of the remark come clear. It almost went unmentioned by me, since it seemed so inconsequential. She, however, pointed out that the information was crucial. Implied was an admonition to me that it was probably useless to spend the necessary time and effort to prepare a grant proposal since the project probably would not appeal to those in Washington who make decisions. Competition for funds is intense. The worries of new black mothers who seek medical care in a teaching hospital is hardly a high priority matter in the eyes of most white persons. (We learned later, it is a priority for some white persons interested in cross-racial adoption.)

Through this and other such incidents, as interpreted by an African American colleague, a white person may begin to see research scholarship in a new light. Most white academics have participated in conversations where well-meaning white faculty speculate about the naïveté of blacks in research. Sometimes kindhearted whites, who are anxious to see minority persons succeed professionally, want to tell black friends that their questions are irrelevant. However, whites are seldom this candid for fear of sounding racist. For most nice white people this distinction between "sounding racist" and being racist is important. When we label our motivation "kindness" we reinforce our belief that we are not personally responsible for or involved in racism. Our rationalization allows us to distance ourselves from a problem we perceive as belonging to others, to whites who are prejudiced and to persons of color who are unduly sensitive and inclined to misinterpret.

In fact, most statements that sound racist *are* racist. It is true that the white faculty members did not want to hurt Ruth's feelings, but kindness is not the only motivation for such white behavior. "Kind" whites are so accustomed to being in power that they do not even consider the depth of the racism implicit in their judgment. They simply take it for granted that any question worth researching is a question that is important to white culture. The irony is that, in the name of "kindness," racism is perpetuated and so are the racist myths about black incompetence.

Another incident on the same project exemplifies a related concern. Our project proposal was presented at a regularly scheduled faculty colloquium in which colleagues gather to criticize members' work in progress. The introduction to the project included a reminder that pregnant women in general have concerns about their ability to mother and about the future of their unborn children. In a society that devalues inherited dark skin color, black mothers worry about their children's future encounters with racism. Therefore, the purpose of the project was to investigate the significance of skin color to mother-infant relationships.

Our colleagues, all white, seemed interested and anxious to be helpful. Some raised questions about the rationale for the project. Was this a child abuse proposal? Do black mothers reject children of certain skin tones? Should the project be viewed as a study on the causes of black family instability? Would the results explain the inability of black males to keep jobs?

As the session progressed Dr. Fuller became increasingly agitated. To me, her reaction seemed unduly intense as she insisted that this was a study of normality, not pathology. My reaction was one I judged as pragmatic, not racist. If pathology sells in the funding market why not mention that our study could contribute to more black family stability? It took her months to make me understand why it was important to her integrity and the integrity of the project to focus on ordinary, "normal" black families. As she explained, most white people automatically assume that "normal" families are white. If whites think of stable black families at all, they are inclined to think of "special" families like the family of Colin Powell. She needed to resist the assumption. The thought of a large aggregate of "normal" black families seemed unlikely and not worthy of research attention. She wanted to educate our white colleagues that it is unfair to assume any study of black families is a study of pathology. Nor would she allow them to assume that normal, nonpathological interactions between mothers and their black babies are not an "important" subject for investigation.

My contribution to our mutual education about interactions between blacks and whites was to explain to her what motivated our associates. They were anxious to see her succeed. As sophisticated researchers themselves, they knew the rules of the funding game. They were trying hard to help her play that game successfully. What they failed to understand was that she wanted to change the rules. Since they were trying so hard to be helpful her anger was both incomprehensible and hurtful.

As this example suggests, when a white person and a person of color work together as equals, the white team member may confront the subtlety of discrimination, perhaps for the first time. The experience may evoke a type of pain and frustration that the white person has seldom, if ever, experienced before—rage at unfair rules coupled with the frustration that comes to persons without the power to make changes.

These incidents become more significant when they are viewed in a larger context. They are an example of that elusive concept, institutional racism. In their book

Organizational Environments: Ritual and Rational, J. W. Meyers and W. R. Scott speak of "rational myths" that identify the purposes of organizations. Institutional beliefs are rational in that they identify the specific social purposes of the organization and specify "in rule-like manner what activities are to be carried out." They are "myths in the sense that they depend for their efficacy . . . on the fact that they are widely shared . . . by individuals or groups that have been granted the right to determine such matters."[11]

In this case, the institution's rational purpose was to serve the entire community well and provide service. The rational rule that applied to its rational belief in nondiscrimination was that all activities were to be carried out fairly without reference to race, color, creed, or national origin. The myths that governed the institution's actions were the widely shared beliefs of the decision makers. In this case the decision makers, almost all white, shared the belief that few black families are free of pathology, but most white families are. This belief led to unnoticed and unintended racism in their thought and action.

Differences in experience and socialization led this black woman to ask questions from a perspective that was foreign to that of her peers. They found it understandably difficult to be interested in questions that had never arisen in their own experience. Unfortunately, too many individuals from the dominant perspective assume that questions from a different perspective are at best "not good" questions and at worst "irrelevant" questions. Therefore, in scholarly decision making, questions raised by a black woman were considered irrelevant. The problem was exacerbated by a difference in gender perspective, since almost all of the decision makers were men. They found it doubly difficult to identify with the concerns of a pregnant black woman. The values that dominate thought patterns of the decision makers differed from those of the researchers.

The reward system in academic medicine is geared to favor those who ask questions within the white, male framework, because that framework is most familiar to traditional power brokers. A central thesis here is that the process of eradicating discrimination in any institution, including the church, can be helped by a study of the rational myths that govern the application of nondiscriminatory rules.

The church might be better served by funding studies of the rational myths that affect the behavior of our decision makers than by funding studies about subjects such as how to restructure the church. We might learn that many of our decisions are governed by unspoken racist myths, like the one about black family pathology. One of my greatest fears about downsizing church bureaucracies is that it will keep us from including a significant number of nonwhite persons on all boards and committees. Is there still a deep-seated myth that white persons, particularly men, are more levelheaded and wise than most persons of color?

WHITES ON THE DEFENSIVE

Most white persons of goodwill are comfortable discussing racism if the discussion is rational rather than emotional, and we have looked at some of the reasons for that. Understanding emotional responses is complex and time consuming. Often it is painful, so most of us shy away from racial encounters in which persons of color show much emotion about white racism.

When faced with accusations about what "your people" have done to "our people," white people respond in one of three ways.

One response is to *offer sympathy.* This response implies a power differential; the white person feels sorry about the bad things that have happened to the person of color. In effect we say, "I can't tell you how sorry I am, how bad I feel for you. If there is anything I (the powerful one) can do for you (the unfortunate one) I will try to do it." There are times when sympathy is an appropriate response. When it is offered in a patronizing tone, however, implying that whites view nonwhites as underprivileged, it is heard as an insult to nonwhite persons. One Latina acquaintance calls this the is-there-anything-I-can-do-to-help? response. The insult may be unintentional, but it is an insult nonetheless. Nonwhite persons do not want to be helped. They want to be listened to, taken seriously, be part of the decision-making structure. The implication is that the white person is willing to be generous in the traditional meaning of *generous*, but is not willing to be the one to make sacrifices.

A second response can be called *the identification response*. In this case the white person asks to be absolved of guilt by taking on a nonwhite identity. Some persons of color tell me that the most offensive phrase a white person (WASP) can speak about racism is to say, "I know just how you feel." Whites should know that is impossible. Any white person who has grown to adulthood in this society simply cannot understand all that it means to be nonwhite in America.

Finally there is *the refutation of guilt response*. It comes in two forms, a soft rejoinder and a hard one. Hard-liner whites say in effect, "I'm not responsible for what my great grandparents did, and you have no right to try to make me feel guilty." The soft responders say in effect, "You don't understand. I have been involved in the civil rights movement all my life. You should not ask me to do more than I am doing already." The other side sometimes refers to this as the but-I-marched-in-Selma response.

How sad it is that we hear each other in such unkind and distrustful ways! Racism on the part of persons of color as well as white people complicates communication too much of the time.

CAN WE ALL DO BETTER?

Given increasing nonwhite rage and escalating white frustration, tension is rising. Numbers of white persons are now saying that they are more uncomfortable and frightened in the intimate presence of persons from other races than they were in an earlier time. Part of our discomfort is the deep, ingrained fear of differences. However, some of the fear stems from our uncertainty about how to behave. We are intimidated by persons of color. We are afraid that however hard we try we will make a mistake, and are frequently told we have.

Therefore well-meaning white persons have developed at least two unproductive patterns of response as we try to develop new rules for a new day in interracial interaction. The first response is to pretend there is no qualitative difference between persons from different racial and ethnic backgrounds. Some well-intentioned white parents tell their children that African American people or Latinos/Latinas or Asian Americans are just like us. Unless one has time and opportunity to expand on this explanation it will be inadequate. We *are* alike in some ways. Shakespeare expressed that sentiment eloquently when Shylock, the moneylender, speaks to his opponents in *The Merchant of Venice*.

> *Shylock:* I am a Jew. Hath not a Jew eyes? Hath not a Jew hands, organs, dimensions, senses, affection, passions; fed with the same food, hurt with the same weapons, subject to the same diseases, healed by the same means, warmed and cooled by the same winter and summer as a Christian is? If you prick us, will we not bleed? If you tickle us, do we not laugh? If you poison us do we not die?[12]

Yet we are not all alike culturally, and we are not treated in the same manner by the social system. It is usually easier for white parents to teach respect for cultural differences

86

than to admit and explain the discriminatory differences. However, a myriad of subtle rules in society make it clear to nonwhites that life is not the same for them as for white citizens. For example, there are powerful, private social groups, such as some country clubs, that still discriminate by policy. Many important economic and political decisions are made in these settings. There are other places such as certain ski, tennis, or golf resorts, restaurants, apartment complexes, and even churches where persons of color are made to feel that they do not "fit in." If they go into such places they must conform rigidly to white ways of speech, dress, and behavior.

White parents who obscure these differences are contributing to their children's misunderstanding of cultural contexts. The least we can do is be honest with ourselves and with our children about the way American society really works. We need more white people who understand the difference between the rules about equal opportunity and the myths by which they are implemented. Understanding can be a first step toward improved interracial relationships.

Another approach being adopted by more and more white persons is withdrawal. We excuse ourselves by saying we know when we are not wanted. People of color do not want "nice white ladies" anymore, so we will just stay as far away from any community of color as we can. We will lock our car doors and keep right on going, having as little contact as possible because whatever we say or do will be wrong. A common example used to illustrate the futility of efforts to communicate cross-racially or cross-culturally is the problem of deciding what words to use to refer to groups of nonwhites. How often we hear, "If you call somebody Hispanic somebody yells at you for not saying Chicano. If you say Chicano they get mad at you for not saying Hispanic. About the time you figure out which of those terms to use somebody tells you both words are insults. You should say Latino or Latina." Since you do not want to offend anybody you just keep your head down and try not to get yourself into interracial situations.

Of course as Christians we cannot put our heads down and avoid the issue. We must risk making mistakes. It takes patience and hard work. How much we are willing to learn about our own racism, as well as our sexism, ageism, and class prejudice, is a function of the way each of us manages the tensions between who we are and who we want to be. We are imperfect and racist by virtue of birth into this society. We want to be nonracist because that is what God calls us to be. We may never attain the goal because racial misunderstanding is such a complex matter. We may never understand completely or recover completely. George Tinker put it this way: "I do not believe that all White Americans are de facto recovering racists. By far most are not at all 'in recovery.' I meant the metaphor as a metaphor for healing, as a way of pointing towards a healing process. The significance of this begins with an acknowledgment that racism, . . . the exercise of white privilege, is an addiction."[13] As Christian white Americans, we need to be aware of our addiction and commit ourselves to a life of recovery. If we do not, the increasing racial tension in our society can only get worse.

A LESSON IN RECOVERY

One final incident illustrates, better than any other, the evolution of my understanding about racism during Ruth Fuller's and my work on our research project. One weekend we had a professional meeting in a resort area. Ruth brought her fifteen-year-old son, Michael, with her. Unfortunately, a bout with the twenty-four-hour flu left me uninterested in attending one of the evening meetings. Ruth went and left Michael with me. Our condominium was quite a distance from the center of the resort area in which the big hotel, fancy restaurants, and expensive shops were located. Michael wanted to see the area, so I drove him over and dropped him off, promising to return about 10:00 P.M.

As the evening wore on my anxiety rose. Michael was a big boy at fifteen, over six feet tall. He was also broad shouldered and very dark of skin. Thoughts of how a black teen, by himself, might be treated in that exclusive, all-white environment began to frighten me. Would a security guard question him? Would he be accused of trying to steal something? Might some fearful white person slap him or push him around just because he was so big and so black? With sweaty palms and pounding heart I returned to the resort center early. There was Michael, sitting on the curb in the same spot where he had been dropped off. Neither of us said much on the way back to the condominium. No inquiries about how he liked the shops, the food, the music. We both understood the trip had been a mistake. Later, when I told his mother the story, she simply smiled and said, "Now you know how I feel every time he leaves the house."

Explaining the intensity of his fear and my anxiety does not lend itself to rational discourse. That is a fundamental flaw in our ability to communicate the meaning of racism. There are no facts to give, no specifics to provide. In point of fact nothing happened. If a white person were to ask me to explain what made me so anxious, there would be nothing tangible to explain. That night I came closer than I have ever come before to understanding how an American person of color feels about white culture. I looked at Michael, sitting silent beside me, and thought about the adulthood that lies ahead for this tall, broad-shouldered young man with very dark skin. Will he become an alienated, angry, and hostile person? I do not know, but if he does I will try not to judge him too harshly.

This lack of concreteness in racially tense encounters leads some white persons to dismiss such incidents as figments of the imagination. Yet our society is being torn apart by racism that mothers and fathers of sons like Michael experience. They are enraged over environments like the resort we visited. And we, the white folks, are either so naïve we do not understand or else so callous we do not want to understand. As Christians we need to try.

SUMMARY

The chapter began with assumptions and boundaries. It was written for well-meaning white persons, not intentionally bigoted ones. It focused on white racism, which is deemed to be a more significant factor in racial tension than nonwhite racism. We did not discuss poverty in an effort to uncouple poverty and race in the minds of white readers. Racism exists without poverty.

We also looked at the traditional rules for white behavior in interracial contexts. In an earlier era nonwhite persons were appreciative of helpful white persons. Today many whites are distressed that traditional patterns of behaving in interracial exchanges no longer produce relaxed, comfortable dialogue. For whites the progress made in the civil rights movement produced unintended consequences. As persons of color have gained some power of their own they are less willing to be grateful for assistance from white people.

We also looked at the subtle ways in which white racism creates institutional racism, particularly through the illustration of my colleague's research project. Whereas the rules of society now require equal treatment for all, implementation of the rules is governed by "myths"—that is, widely held assumptions shared by institutional decision makers. Some of those myths are inherently racist.

Whites are adapting to changed patterns of racial communication, but some of the adaptations are not altogether adequate. Neither ignoring differences nor withdrawing from interracial dialogue will solve our problems. The issues are complex, but Christians are summoned to try, even in the face of discomfort and difficulty.

FOR REFLECTION

1. Do you agree or disagree with George Tinker, who says that all white persons in America are racists?

2. Describe a "minority" experience in your own life, a time when you felt that you were being treated as an outsider because you were "different."

3. How do you deal with your anger when you have an experience in which you feel you are being stereotyped rather than being judged on your own merit?

NOTES

1. "And now, a word or two about the future," a fact sheet compiled by the Anti-Defamation League of Denver, 1996. Sources are cited by publication name only.

Center for Immigration studies: By the year 2000, one-third of all U.S. citizens will be people of color.

1990 U.S. Census: Since 1980 the Asian population of the United States has more than doubled. The Hispanic population grew by more than 50 percent, the African American population grew by 30 percent.

2. George Tinker is Associate Professor of Cross Cultural Ministries at the Iliff School of Theology, Denver, Colorado.

3. Jim Wallis, *The Soul of Politics,* A Harvest Book (San Diego: Harcourt Brace & Co., 1995), p. 95.

4. Cynthia B. Astle, "Is Torched Churches Furor a Hoax?" *United Methodist Reporter,* August 23, 1996, p. 4.

5. Ibid.

6. Wanda Coleman, "Get Out of Dodge!" UTNE Reader, May/June 1994, no. 63, p. 103. This article first appeared in *The Nation.*

7. Spike Lee's thought-provoking movie about racial interactions in urban America ends in defeat and violence. The audience is left with uncertainty when so many well-meaning characters lose their battle for civility.

8. After serving as project director for a National Institutes of Mental Health grant at the hospital, I continued as a member of the clinical faculty. In that capacity I worked on various research projects with Ruth L. Fuller, M.D. At that time Dr. Fuller was director of the Community Psychiatry program.

9. Much of this material appeared earlier as a journal article. Sally B. Geis and Ruth L. Fuller, "Inadvertent Discrimination in Medical Research," *Journal of Religion and Health* (vol. 29, no. 3), Fall 1990, pp. 207-17.

10. George Tinker, notes made in response to an earlier draft of this chapter, September 6, 1996.

11. J. W. Meyers and W. R. Scott, *Organizational Environments: Ritual and Rational* (Beverly Hills, Calif.: Sage Press, 1983), p. 14.

12. William Shakespeare, *The Merchant of Venice,* Act III, sc. 1.

13. Tinker, notes.

CHAPTER FOUR

The Irrelevance of Restructuring

The preceding chapters have focused on discord within the Christian community. Chapter 1 concentrated on the conflict related to divergent meanings for the terms *family*, or *Christian values*. Chapter 2 analyzed the reasons for the controversy and gave suggestions for resolution. Chapter 3 directed attention toward the friction between white persons and persons of color with particular emphasis on the role white persons play in exacerbating that struggle.

This chapter differs from the preceding chapters in a number of ways. Readers may not immediately see the connection between a discussion of church structure and the primary focus of the book, which is the transformation of our divided Christian factions into a community of greater health and wholeness. Careful examination, however, suggests an integral relationship. Restructuring is a primary technique by which institutionalized denominational bodies are seeking to address the erosion of public confidence in the ability of mainstream Christians to impact society's ills. Suppose we find that the questions being asked about restructuring, and the plans developed out of the answers to those questions are insufficient for renewal? Then there is an obligation to include the issue of restructuring as part of the analysis within this book.

SIGNS OF DISINTEGRATION

Bemoaning the state of institutionalized religion is a favorite topic for church watchers, both those who are members of communities of faith and those who are not. Even political figures are writing about what is wrong in religion. In an effort to respond to their eroding status in society, many denominational bodies are restructuring in the hope that streamlining their operations will help restore their public image. Legislation to facilitate reorganization is being passed in general assemblies of many mainline denominations. For example, the Evangelical Lutheran Church in America, the Presbyterian Church U.S.A., the African American Episcopal Zion Church, and The United Methodist Church are all in the throes of restructuring. Plans are being developed to revamp general church agencies, and workshops abound on how to refocus the local church.

These plans include an attempt to change the focus or vision of what churches should be and do. Those of us who have sat in mainline pews most of our lives are becoming familiar with a new vocabulary for change, as a new set of action verbs becomes familiar. We are being asked to revision, reimagine, reengineer, reinvent our communities of faith. Leaders of the fix-it movement have also introduced us to the concept of *paradigm shifts.* (I will explain this term later.) We are told that either the church is in the midst of a paradigm shift (judged good by some and bad by others) or else we are in need of a paradigm shift. Many church executives are turning to business and industry to learn about paradigm shifts as well as about organizational management.

Efforts to respond to the perceived crisis are understandable. Most of society agrees that all is not well in mainline churches. Membership is down. Prestige in the secular world has eroded. In the 1960s it was taken for granted that references to God and country referred to Christianity and the U.S.A. Christianity was understood as a mix of Robert Bellah's "civil religion"[1] and membership in a mainline denomination, preferably Episcopalian or Presbyterian.

Obviously much has changed since then. Religious pluralism is a fact of religious life in America. Womanist theology and feminist scholarship have been legitimated in most U.S. schools of theology. The critical analytic stance of postmodernism has altered the way some Christians interpret scripture. As I suggested in the introduction, judgments about the value of those changes depends on the theological and ideological perspective of the person making the judgment. Viewed through liberal eyes much of the change has been good. Seen through conservative eyes many of these changes are dangerous, the causes of our decay. If not stopped, they spell disaster.

However, as we learned in the introduction, some problems worry both conservatives and liberals. Though a smattering of mainline churches have vital programs for children and youth, congregations in mainline churches are aging. This leads some futurists to predict there will soon be nobody in mainline churches on Sunday but old people. Local church finance committees express increasing concern over changing priorities in resource allocation. Clergy pensions, health and liability insurance now command a larger percent of the budget than do the program ministries of many churches.[2] Some local church leaders suggest the day may not be far off when the cost of membership in a denominational body is not worth the services it provides. This is a discouraging picture.

These specific church-related problems float in a cultural sea viewed by many as a society of decaying values and failed ethical standards. Church members worry along with the rest of the population about crumbling families and family values, deteriorating business ethics, media violence, and the environmental crisis. Yet the church seems unable to exert much influence over the ethical and moral chaos in which we find ourselves. Is denominational main-line religion, like the dinosaurs, doomed to extinction?

RULES FOR FIXING BROKEN THINGS

No doubt changes must be made in outmoded habit patterns within the church. But how? Perhaps some answers can be found in my rural background. During each summer of my childhood, we spent some time on the family farm in western Kansas. In those days if something broke you fixed it yourself or went without, so we learned a lot about fixing broken things. The first rule for fixing malfunctioning equipment was one articulated eloquently in Robert Pirsig's *Zen and the Art of Motorcycle Maintenance*.[3] On the farm it meant that before you started taking things apart, you looked long and carefully at the object that needed repair. Before you removed or changed anything, you had to be sure you knew how the parts went together and how they affected one another. Would removing one particular screw detach something vital, something that should not be detached? Only careful preparation and full understanding of the machine could ensure that the person doing the repairs would avoid the danger of making things worse instead of better—a lesson many of us have learned the hard way in disreputable auto repair shops. For us today, in our eagerness to solve denominational problems, we need to stop and ask ourselves whether we are spending enough time and effort studying how churches actually work before we begin taking things apart. If we are not doing that, the repairs to church structure may not make things any better than they were in the past. A pessimist might even suggest that things could get worse.

The second rule on the farm was the familiar phrase, "If it ain't broke, don't fix it." Before you started repairing anything, you had to be sure that it was truly broken. Most repair persons, including my washer repairman, can relate countless stories of persons who call for repair only to find that something was not connected properly or that a battery needed to be replaced—no repair service was necessary. If the customer had made a careful assessment of the problem, she or he could have saved a sizable bill. Could it be that solving the contemporary problems of church life does not require tearing structures apart and putting them back together? Maybe something is disconnected and all we need to do is plug it back in. It may be the institutional church is not working because it is no longer plugged in to the circuit that gives it life. Perhaps we have become disconnected from our source of energy, the gospel of justice and mercy that we hear read each Sunday but fail to comprehend.

The third rule on the farm came from Uncle Clyde, who used to say as he pondered a malfunctioning tractor, windmill, milk separator, or electric generator, "Sally Ann, remember—you don't go to fixin' nothin' till you're sure what's broke and why'd it break right *there*." The longer I watched him the better I understood. Some things break at the point of greatest outside stress, other things break because of a weakness in the original design that does not allow the object to withstand normal stress. Before my uncle began to fix anything, he needed to know which problem he faced so he could design his repair to fit the *real* problem. It was not enough to simply patch the break. Usually a good repair required more. Sometimes he needed to reinforce a weak spot in whatever was broken. At other times he needed to readjust the outside force that was causing undue stress on the object that broke.

Herein lies my greatest anxiety about the amount of money and energy now being devoted to church restructuring. Probably churches do need to streamline bureaucracy, eliminate needless duplication of effort, cut down on paperwork. Yet we may be so focused on what is wrong inside the church that we are not paying enough attention to stresses from the outside. Problems such as racism and greed that are destroying not only our churches but also our whole society may not be affected by restructuring the church. Are we rearranging the furniture while ignoring the floodwaters rising at the end of our street?

Most restructuring discussion is held among the white, aging, middle-class persons who now hold the majority of leadership roles in mainline denominations. Those of us who belong to that leadership and participate in these discussions must ask tough questions. How does changing committee structure help Christians respond better to the world in which, as Jim Wallis reminds us, "Tonight, the urban children of the world's only remaining superpower will go to bed to the sound of gunfire"[4]? Lucy Loomis or Linda Geis, physicians who see the children of the rural poor as well as the urban poor, would probably add that the children are not only frightened but hungry, and too many of their illnesses go unattended for lack of insurance.[5]

THINKING ABOUT PARADIGM SHIFTS

Today's mainline church leadership acknowledges that something is wrong with our vision. However, articulating a new vision seems difficult. One way to discuss changing vision, as well as structure, is to speak of paradigm shifts.

The church's understanding of paradigms comes primarily from consultants in business and industry who have adapted the concept as a tool for management. Joel Barker deserves credit for popularizing the concept.[6] In the 1980s he developed a number of provocative videotapes and articles in which he illustrated the ways in which preconceived understandings about the meaning of information result in misinterpretation or disregard for important data. Barker credits Thomas Kuhn[7] with the basic concept, but it is Barker's interpretation that intrigues management personnel, including church officials.

Barker uses vivid illustrations to demonstrate the ways in which our taken-for-granted assumptions about how the world works (paradigms) blind us from seeing what is really happening. In one of his most quoted video sequences, a woman is seen driving a car at high speed on a country road. She startles an oncoming driver by careening around a curve, barely missing a collision with his car. As she passes, she yells one word out her window at the other driver: "Pig!" The disconcerted driver yells back, "Cow!" intending to trade one insult for another. However, as he rounds the corner he comes face-to-face with a real pig standing in the middle of the road! Suddenly he realizes that the set of assumptions on which he based his response to her warning caused him to respond in an inappropriate manner. Had he understood that she swerved to avoid the pig and was trying to warn him of the upcoming danger, he would have responded to her differently. He would also have turned his attention to avoiding a collision with the pig.

Is there any clergyperson preaching today who could not make a sermon illustration out of that vignette?

Barker's illustrations are helpful explanations of our human tendency to project past experience and assumptions (our old paradigms) onto new situations that can be better understood if we take a fresh view (shift to a new paradigm). Several of them describe powerful business institutions that failed to accept new technology and therefore lost out on new opportunities, or management officials who lacked the imagination to see the potential value of change. They assumed the future would be like the past. Ways of working that were successful yesterday and today would be successful tomorrow, they thought. While they went on doing things in the same old way, conditions for the industry in which they were involved changed drastically. Management's failure to make changes and embrace new ideas has caused some companies that once dominated the market to shut down or at least operate from a badly crippled financial position. A classic case is the Swiss watchmakers who were unwilling to accept the concept of the digital watch and lost their market to the Japanese. Another example is the Eastman Kodak camera company, which was uninterested in the Polaroid process and paid for the mistake with the loss of valuable business. Each of these events was caused by the inability of persons in decision-making positions to "change lenses" or shift paradigms and see the potential in a radically new way of doing business.

CAN THE CHURCH BE COMPARED TO MICROSOFT?

Many leaders within the church see these businesses as analogous to religious denominations. They are intrigued with this new insight about changing lenses (or paradigms) as a way to solve denominational ills. The concept has merit. My criticism of the church's current emphasis on structural change does not stem from a desire to return to old ways of doing things, nor is it part of the ongoing debate about whether change is good or bad. Reverend Lynn Scott, who travels across the country consulting with local church groups, described the debate well when she observed that she finds ardent supporters for each of two attitudes toward the church and change. One group thinks the church is changing too fast. The other thinks it is not changing fast enough. My response to both sides is *yes!* Some changes seem to be coming too slowly. For example, too many mainline churches still create church school programs as if two parents with a couple of children represent the average American family. Yet other changes may be coming too quickly. Some denominations are eliminating membership quotas that require the representation of women and minorities on denominational policy-making boards and agencies. This is done in the name of streamlining bureaucracy, but it will bring other, negative results by intensifying the concentration of church power in the hands of the already powerful.

However, my primary concern is not about the speed of change. I am concerned, rather, about the kind and quality of some changes currently occurring. Is this emphasis on changes in management style and structure being over-sold? We need to consider the weaknesses as well as the strengths of equating the church's problems with those faced by businesses trying to survive in a market economy. It is troublesome to find that some church leaders assume that business management techniques are sufficient tools by which to develop adequate responses to the problems facing Christians at the beginning of the twenty-first century. Some of the management language being used in the church today suggests that we may be dangerously close to suggesting that the development of a large, affluent, and powerful institution like Microsoft is our goal for the Christian community of faith.

CHANGE IS INEVITABLE, NEW VISION IS IMPERATIVE

To be anxious about the church's emphasis on institutional restructure and management techniques is not the same as resisting the concept of paradigm shifts. On the contrary, the concept of a paradigm shift is a powerful one if it is fully understood. Rather than eliminating it, we in the church should study its meaning more carefully. It may offer us great insight into the meaning of our current situation in which our world seems to be breaking apart in unpreventable ways. The type of change we are experiencing was described by Thomas Kuhn in the book he published almost forty years ago, the book Barker credits with giving him his initial understanding of paradigm shifts. Therefore, before we uncritically accept the management application of the term we should learn more about its origins.

WHAT IS A PARADIGM SHIFT?

Scholars interested in the philosophy of science and the sociology of knowledge began talking excitedly about paradigms after the 1962 publication of Thomas S. Kuhn's book *The Structure of Scientific Revolutions*.[8] In the preface of his landmark publication Kuhn defines the term *paradigm*, and discusses what led him to his new insights. One unexpected influence was his spending a year of uninterrupted time devoted to research in a community of social scientists. The situation, he wrote,

> confronted me with unanticipated problems about the difference between such communities and those of the natural scientists among whom I had trained. . . . I was struck by the number and extent of the overt disagreements between social scientists about the nature of legitimate scientific problems and methods. Both history and acquaintance made me doubt that practitioners of the natural sciences possess firmer or more permanent answers to such questions than their colleagues in the social sciences. Yet somehow, the practices of astronomy, physics . . . fail to evoke the controversies over fundamentals that today often seem endemic among say, psychologists or sociologists. Attempting to discover the source of that difference led me to recognize the role in scientific research of what I have since called "paradigms." These I take to be *universally recognized scientific achievements that for a time provide model problems and solutions to a community of practitioners* [italics mine].[9]

Kuhn would probably be surprised that his work on paradigms has been applied to the revitalizing of dying institutions or to the management of for-profit businesses and industries! He wanted to discover *why* and *how* great revolutions in thinking shake the world, particularly the major breakthroughs in the physical sciences that change what people accept as "true." To say it a different way, Kuhn sought to understand how scientists develop new theories that cause whole societies to "shift paradigms," to accept new explanations of phenomena that had previously seemed unexplainable by using information considered invalid in the old paradigm.

The "unanticipated problem," as Kuhn described it, of the differences in communities that first started his thought process may be even more important than the excellent questions he asked about science. He tells us he was struck by the difference between the natural and social science communities. Since he did not believe natural scientists had any firmer grip on the truth than did social scientists, he needed to ask why there were such arguments within the social science community about the nature of legitimate scientific problems as well as about the methods to solve the problems. It would have been helpful to some of us if Kuhn had focused more on the differences between the natural and social science communities than he did. But that was not his major interest.

My presumption is that investigations by social scientists, like those of church leaders, are more influenced by personal values than are the investigations of natural scientists. This is not to suggest that natural science is value free. Natural science data, however, does seem less vulnerable to value judgment than does social science data. For example, Isaac Newton is said to have experienced his insight into the nature of gravity when he was hit on the head by an apple as it fell from a tree. If physicists viewed that story as true because it was part of a sacred canon of science, there might have been more resistance to Albert Einstein's newer theory. Newton's work was judged to be true only because it could be proved empirically.

On the other hand, social scientists work with human behavior, feelings, emotions, and opinions. These are more apt to cloud the ability of scholars to view new or overlooked data objectively. The problem affects public acceptance as well. Many of Kuhn's ideas are relevant to the church, and we would do well to study his thought. Trying to apply his method of analysis to the problems of the church raises certain questions. For example, why do some people begin to question the state of knowledge and challenge the system of authority as they look for new answers? Why does a society accept certain scientific discoveries so quickly? Who refuses to accept the discoveries and why? This last question's meaning in the church is intriguing.

A PARADIGM SHIFT THAT SHOOK THE WORLD

The best way to describe Kuhn's concept of paradigm shift is to give an example. For centuries intelligent people, including the church fathers, believed the earth was at the center of the universe. Then at a particular time in history, and in a relatively short time span, most of the world accepted a totally new understanding of reality. Descriptions of a three-tiered universe still exist in the Bible, but in today's world such descriptions are judged to be allegorical. However, the change in viewpoint did not come without a struggle. Anyone interested in understanding the process of paradigm shifts as Kuhn understood them will do well to read or attend a performance of Bertolt Brecht's play *Galileo*. It dramatizes the story of Galileo Galilei, the man who looked out into space with his new telescope and recognized that the earth orbited around the sun. His discovery of Jupiter's moons and his new theories shook not only the scientific community but the religious community as well. In one scene Galileo is called before the church fathers in Rome who are concerned about his interpretation of what he has seen through his new glass. Here are some excerpts from scene 6:

> *Galileo:* In his blindness man is liable to misread not only the sky but also the Bible.
> *Bellarmin:* The interpretation of the Bible is a matter for the ministers of God.... (*Galileo remains silent.*) The Holy Office has decided that the theory according to which the earth goes around the sun is foolish, absurd, and a heresy. I am ... cautioning you to abandon these teachings.
> *Galileo:* But the facts! . . . The future of all scientific research is . . .
> *Bellarmin (cutting in):* It is not given to man to know the truth: it is granted to him to seek after the truth.[10]

Galileo tried in vain to entice the church fathers to look through his glass to see for themselves what was going on in the "heavens." In the end the church fathers declined. Looking was too dangerous. Suppose they did see something that upset their nicely constructed worldview? Without even looking at his data the church passed judgment on Galileo and forced him to recant. In the eyes of the church, Galileo used the wrong data, and the authority of all Christendom would be threatened beyond repair if he were allowed to publicize his findings. Today we find their behavior foolish and smugly assume we would have been wiser. But would we?

Maybe God is calling leaders of contemporary Western Christianity to a paradigm shift. Maybe God wants us to look into our world and see the economic disparity, the environmental destruction, the glamorized violence that are legitimated by our society, and then to change our perspective. Is it too dangerous to act on that information? Must the data be ignored if we white American Christians are to keep our world intact? Suppose the paradigm shift will require significant changes in our lifestyles. Who is willing to sacrifice?

Perhaps we would rather not look. It might be too dangerous. Are there Galileos in our midst? Are there Christian spokespersons of our time calling us to new vision, using information we wish to ignore? If there are, they are not management advisers. Most are not even church leaders, but some are—we think of Desmond Tutu or Mother Teresa. They ask us to look around us. They ask us to go into our prisons, our public hospitals, and housing projects. If we go, will we really listen to the young mothers with sick children, alienated young men without work, old persons living in isolated walk-up flats? If we considered this information the most important information Christians possess, how would we structure the church?

HOW DO PARADIGM SHIFTS EFFECT RESTRUCTURING?

Paradigm shifts are brought about by new theories that make use of data heretofore overlooked in order to explain phenomena in one of two new ways. Either the new theory explains something that has never been explained before or the new theory explains something more clearly than it has been explained before.

Kuhn's work suggests that new paradigms are created by persons who realize that the accepted explanation of some phenomenon or process is not sufficient. They are troubled when the explanations authorities offer for common occurrences, such as the "rising" of the sun each day, do not reflect accurately the process by which the event takes place. Through careful observation, such individuals with fine minds begin intensive investigation of the events that interest him or her. Consider Pasteur, who was dissatisfied with contemporary explanations of the causes of disease. He used new technology, the microscope, to help him look in new places to find a new answer. He discovered a world of creatures too small to be observed by the human eye. With his newfound information he was able to explain things that had never been explainable before, and the paradigm shifted.

Pasteur's discovery was not produced by the restructuring of medicine. The restructuring of medical science was the *result* of Pasteur's discovery, not its *cause*. When Pasteur pointed medical science to a new source of data, it was obvious that restructuring had to take place in order to accommodate both new methodology and new information. Ultimately, work in microbiology, as well as other related sciences, has revolutionized the practice of medicine. Today physicians are dependent on an vast array of equipment and personnel trained to gather useful information in many fields. Almost all patient treatment is predicated on laboratory tests, x ray, or CAT scan images, as well as a host of other sophisticated information-gathering techniques.

NEW QUESTIONS, NEW FOCUS

Armed with a fuller understanding of paradigm shifts than is provided in management literature, we can ask new questions about what changes need to be made in the church. In the introduction I suggested that the quality of the questions we ask determines the quality of the answers we receive. Basing our questions on Kuhn's work may lead us to ask some helpful ones. Here are some we might try.

1. What new theory that makes use of heretofore overlooked information or new information is guiding our restructuring?

We need to think carefully about this question, for the answer does not seem obvious. Data about our eroding membership and loss of prestige are certainly not new or overlooked information. They are the facts we have worried about for a couple of decades.

For all the talk about paradigm shifts, there does not seem to be a satisfactory answer to our question in church literature about restructure. Perhaps our effort to solve the problems through restructuring is, in itself, evidence that we are stuck in an old paradigm. We know that our current paradigm, our way of using the data we think is important, is not producing particularly satisfactory results. However, we seem to lack a Galileo or a Pasteur to show us a new way to look at our world. Or is there a Galileo knocking at our door whom we fail to invite into our conversation because her or his ideas are too dangerous, too radical?

2. *Who resists the acceptance of the fundamental changes in the understanding of information that causes paradigm shifts?*

History suggests the persons most apt to resist new knowledge are those who hold the most power and receive the most benefits in the traditional paradigm. Such persons are seldom capable of accepting radically new ways of looking at data because the current system works well for them. Women may suggest that the church hierarchy's treatment of feminist theologians and wisdom literature is an example of this principle. Numerous powerful patriarchs have condemned their work as "the Sophia movement" and called it heresy. Could incidents such as this be the beginning of a true paradigm shift?

3. *What stresses are causing us to look for a new paradigm?*

F. Thomas Trotter, former president of Alaska University and General Secretary of the United Methodist Board of Higher Education and Ministry, says that if you want to know how the church will restructure, watch the hot spots.[11] Hot spots are the points of friction between traditional and nontraditional perceptions of Christian community. Today's list would include such issues as full acceptance of homosexual persons; support for safe abortions; free health care and education for all children, including illegal immigrant children; acceptance of nonsexist language in biblical translations and in liturgies of the church; greater emphasis on ethnic ministries, including Native Americans, Latinos, African Americans, and Asian Americans.

Those who advocate acceptance of these changes ask that we give high priority to data that some chose to overlook. They are troubled by inconsistencies between church theory and practice. The church talks of justice and love for all persons, yet there seems to be little evidence that we are serious about affecting the economic and sociopolitical structures of our day.

Passions run high, however, among persons with differing opinions about these issues, and tensions run so deep that some scholarly observers, such as James Davison Hunter,[12] refer to the contemporary dispute among persons within the American Judeo-Christian tradition as a culture war.

My judgment is that conservatives are correct, at least in the short run. This foment is dangerous to the well-being of contemporary religious institutions. Yet in the long run this time of unraveling and breaking apart that we are experiencing within the Christian community may be essential for the ultimate health of the Christian faith. As persons with varying perspectives vie for power in denominational bodies, the new community story is unfolding.

ARE CONDITIONS RIGHT FOR A PARADIGM SHIFT?

According to Kuhn, the exposure of inconsistencies between theory and practice, even when it brings serious disagreement in a given community, is a good sign. In Galileo's world the technology for shipbuilding had become sophisticated enough that vessels were capable of going farther than the men who navigated them felt they could safely sail. Some navigators feared that going too far might put them at risk of sailing off the end of the earth. The most adventuresome sailors, however, were beginning to suspect that there were places ships could safely sail even when they no longer had the north star by which to navigate. They reasoned there must be a way to navigate the new waters, but how? Into this world, already aware of its urgent need for better explanations of the movement of heavenly bodies, came a man with a new way of looking.

ARE WE PREPARED FOR A RADICAL NEW DAY?

How shall we prepare ourselves for a paradigm shift if we give credence to the analysis presented here? First we must free ourselves from the idea that we can control or manage a genuine paradigm shift so that it will "make things better" in ways that we already understand. If we are to embrace Kuhn's ideas about paradigm shifts, we may be called to give up some ideas as dear to us as the idea of a three-tiered universe was to the church fathers of an earlier time.

We must also understand that nobody yet knows how to predict exactly when or where a breakthrough will come. However, there is every indication that we should be looking and listening for the new voice or voices that are changing the church.

ACCEPTING INFORMATION PREVIOUSLY IGNORED MAY BE CHANGING US NOW

It is possible that we are living in the midst of a major paradigm shift. As with most paradigm shifts, the new way of thinking works its way into the halls of power from the outside. My guess is that no paradigm shift will be created by a denominational planning committee. The revolutionary shaking of Christianity's foundations will come from outsiders like the women in the Catholic church demanding equal status, gay and lesbian persons insisting on equal treatment and respect, persons in the two-thirds of the world who criticize the U.S. churches for the economic greed we seem to condone as public and private business policy.

Insider efforts to restructure denominations will not be particularly helpful in addressing these large, long-term issues. In the short run it may make denominations more efficient and responsive to local needs. In the long run I doubt that restructuring will make much difference.

WILL WE ACCEPT OR RESIST NEW INSIGHTS?

Most of the common citizens within the church have an intuitive feeling that the road ahead will be rough. We may be right. We may never return to the glorious days of the 1950s and 1960s when mainline churches enjoyed unprecedented growth and prestige. That may be all right. A radically new form of Christendom may serve humanity better than the one we have now. It may not come in my lifetime, but it may be needed and may eventually come, whether we like it or not. My advice is that we listen carefully to those on the fringe of the church. Some of our mainline insider-outsiders are radically liberal. Others are radically conservative. Most of them are real outsiders to institutionalized religion. They are Christians we hardly know in mainline churches because they do not speak our language. They are the poor of our inner cities, many of whom are fundamentalists and Pentecostal. All of us on the inside of mainline churches will find one outsider group or another difficult to hear.

Folklore tells us that Albert Einstein once was asked how he made his discovery about the relationship of time and space. He is said to have answered, "I dreamed I stood in a new place. Newton sat under the apple tree, looked up, and saw the apple fall. I dreamed I stood outside the world and looked back at it from afar." That may be what we are hearing when these outsider Christians say with excitement, "Please, come stand where I am standing. Let me tell you about new ways to understand the story of Christ crucified, Christ risen, the Christ who came that we might have life and have it more abundantly."

THE IRONY FOR CHRISTIANS

When contemplating a *real* paradigm shift in Christendom, we who live within the traditional church feel anxiety and fear coupled with excitement and anticipation. We are frightened because we realize that if our paradigm shift follows the course that Kuhn describes, it will be painful, particularly for persons who are steeped in traditional ways of thinking about God, about the role of the church in the world, about our own denominations.

Yet we know there are some things that "do not fit" between what the church does and what Jesus called his followers to do and to be. So we are excited because we believe that if we can learn significant new ways of viewing our Christian calling, we can be better disciples.

For Christians there is something painfully familiar about this story of ridicule and rejection when radical new ideas about human behavior are advanced. Our basic Gospel story is about a paradigm shifter who was such an outsider, he was born in a barn with a dirt floor.

Think of the things he said about the past paradigm. "You have heard that it was said to the men of old . . . but I say to you . . ." (Matt. 5:21-22). And for his speaking and teaching, for advancing radical new ideas, this man we call the Christ, the Son of God, was crucified.

From the beginning, God's ministry has proved to be difficult for humans to understand and perform. Probably our current predicament is neither greater nor smaller than ones faced by the church in the past. The church is always broken in that it is never a perfect reflection of God's desire. It's just that sometimes we notice. It is clear that planning restructure without new vision will be unproductive.

SUMMARY

We began this chapter by describing denominational leadership's effort to respond to contemporary church problems by revisioning or restructuring. We reviewed some "Rules for Repair" and cautioned that unless one is clear about what is broken and why the break occurred, the efforts to repair may not be useful.

Then we looked at the popularity of applying business management techniques as solutions to denominational problems, and questioned their suitability. It is doubtful that the origin of the church's current problems is internal to church organizations. Rearranging the furniture within our religious houses does little to respond to the chaos outside the church. What we need is a new paradigm.

Paradigms, a word first used by scientist Thomas Kuhn, are theories that become universally recognized explanations of heretofore unexplained phenomenon. Galileo and Pasteur are examples of persons whose discoveries changed the structures of their societies. Kuhn called these radical reorganizations "paradigm shifts." Persons such as they, persons with new vision, seldom come from within the established realm of power. Usually they are outsiders, who see data formerly overlooked and ignored as unimportant. So the question is, Are there outsiders to whom we in the church should be listening? Are they the people who will give vision to a new structure and cause a true paradigm shift?

In the final chapter we will revisit a question from scripture referred to in the introduction. Faced with all the problems and complexities addressed in this book, we may feel overwhelmed. Each citizen Christian must ultimately ask the question Nicodemus asked Jesus, "How can a man be born when he is old? Can he enter a second time into his mother's womb and be born?" (John 3:4).

FOR REFLECTION

1. The chapter suggests that restructuring is not the best way to revitalize an organization. Recall your own experience with restructuring within your church or workplace. What did you expect it to do? Were your expectations met?

2. Lynn Scott says she hears from two groups of persons in the church: those who think things are changing too fast and those who think they are not changing fast enough. To which group do you belong? Why do you feel that way?

3. This chapter suggests that true paradigm shifts spring from new ideas or theories. These are almost always developed by outsiders rather than by insiders. Can you think of any radical shifts in institutional religion that have taken place in your lifetime?

If yes, were they caused by insiders or outsiders?

If no, do you think it is good or bad that there have been no radical changes?

NOTES

1. Robert Bellah, *Varieties of Civil Religion*, 1st ed. (San Francisco: Harper & Row, 1980).

2. See "Multiply God's Love," prepared for the United Methodist General Conference, April 1996, by the General Council on Finance and Administration of The United Methodist Church in cooperation with United Methodist Communication Service, p. 28.

3. Robert M. Pirsig, *Zen and the Art of Motorcycle Maintenance: An Inquiry into Values* (New York: William Morrow, 1974), pp. 71-72.

4. Jim Wallis, *The Soul of Politics*, p. xiii.

5. Dr. Loomis is a family physician practicing in the Neighborhood Health Clinics, Denver General Hospital. Dr. Geis codirects a clinic for children without health insurance in Ft. Collins, Colorado.

6. Joel Barker, "Business of Paradigms," rev. ed. (Minneapolis: ChartHouse, 1989).

7. Thomas S. Kuhn, *The Structure of Scientific Revolutions*, 2nd ed. (Chicago: University of Chicago Press, 1970).

8. Thomas S. Kuhn, *The Structure of Scientific Revolutions* (Chicago: University of Chicago Press 1962). A second, enlarged edition was published in 1970.

9. Kuhn (1962), p. viii.

10. Bertolt Brecht, "Galileo," *Seven Plays by Bertolt Brecht* (New York: Grove Press, 1961), scene 6, pp. 363-64.

11. Dr. Trotter has given me this advice in numerous private conversations, the most recent of which occurred at the United Methodist General Conference, April 1996.

12. James Davison Hunter, *Culture Wars: The Struggle to Define America* (New York: Basic Books, 1990).

CHAPTER FIVE

More Thoughts on Being Born Again

And let us not grow weary in well-doing, for in due season we shall reap, if we do not lose heart. (Gal. 6:9)

In the introduction I asked, Can the contemporary, mainline American church be transformed into a more hopeful and vibrant influence on the communities and cultures in which we live? The answer will be yes, only if all of us who belong to those churches gain more insight into the task before us. Asking better questions will help us find better answers. My goal has been to raise some new questions and encourage others to do the same. The story of Jesus' conversation with Nicodemus provides a metaphor for the transformation and rebirth we hope to undergo (John 3:1-17). "Truly, truly, I say to you, unless one is born anew, he cannot see the kingdom of God" (John 3:3). My lay interpretation of the story focuses on social justice as well as on personal salvation. One stereotype from which American Christians need to be freed is the assumption that liberals are interested only in social justice and conservatives are interested only in personal salvation. I am assuming that all of us are concerned about both.

IDENTIFYING WITH NICODEMUS

The central figure in our metaphor is Nicodemus. If we assume it is legitimate for us to identify with him, we can project his image into our late-twentieth-century context and learn an important lesson. He was a religious bureaucrat of privileged class. Scripture tells us he was "a man of the Pharisees . . . a ruler of the Jews" (John 3:1). So he was much like many of us who give leadership to mainline Protestant denominations. He held high status in his society and probably lived well. He was not a man of poverty. He was a member of the powerful religious bureaucracy, and was undoubtedly deeply involved in the politics and decision making of institutionalized religion. One would assume that he represented tradition and stability. Yet he dared to seek out this strange young teacher who seemed to be challenging much of what was going on in the religious establishment of his day.

We who are old-timers in the church can project our own situation onto Nicodemus. Many of us have given a lifetime of commitment to the system, to the denominational establishment, to our local churches. We can picture Nicodemus as discouraged and worried about his religious community just as we are about ours. We understand why he went searching for this strange young man who spoke so critically about the state of the religious establishment. As we read his story some of us may wonder whether Nicodemus was as weary as we are of the position he found himself in much of the time. Was he asked to defend his establishment, just as we are, even though we know in our hearts that there are serious problems?

Instead of pushing those thoughts out of his mind and doing business as usual, Nicodemus went seeking answers, as do we. At the time we are introduced to him, Nicodemus may also have been concerned about the way the religious officials were treating this poorly educated maverick. The young man seemed so arrogant and sure of himself. He spoke so strangely and had so little respect for those in authority. Many of the Pharisees believed Jesus was dangerous and needed to be silenced. Obviously the fellow was a real radical whose ideas made most conventional people uneasy. However, Nicodemus had heard reports of some of the things this Jesus said, and they made sense. Perhaps he had heard that this upstart had the nerve to challenge even Scripture. "You have heard that it was said, 'You shall love your neighbor and hate your enemy.' But I say to you, Love your enemies and pray for those who persecute you" (Matt. 5:43-44). Comments such as this were unsettling but seemed authentic. Nicodemus reasoned the man must be of God, or he could not do and say the things he was reported to be doing and saying.

Occasionally one of *us* crosses paths with a radical who seems dangerous but also makes sense. Perhaps a conservative reader has met a "radical" feminist or a gay activist who seemed much more rational than expected. One conservative United Methodist leader told me how surprised he was to finally meet Julian Rush, one of the first in his denomination to "come out" by telling persons in the church he served that he was gay. Many conservatives perceive Julian Rush as a radical leader in a dangerous revolution. In fact Reverend Rush is mild mannered and always meticulously groomed and soft spoken. His passion is providing care for persons living with AIDS. Some conservatives who have visited his clinic have been surprised by his dedication and have been tempted to give financial support to his compassionate work.

A liberal clergywoman, active in the pro-choice movement, told me that she recently met an activist in the right-to-life movement. The person turned out to be a geneticist who is concerned that acceptance of abortion will alter our culture in ways we do not understand. Her argument is that the time will soon come when scientists will be able to read most of the genetic composition of a fetus. For example, we may be able to know which diseases the person will have in his or her lifetime, whether the person will be gay or straight, highly intelligent or rather dull. It may also be possible to develop the "designer fetus." Parents can then choose the characteristics they wish their child to have. The right-to-life activist says that if the church does not make it clear that abortion is wrong, our society may decide it is all right to abort fetuses with characteristics they do not want. Comments like these gave my liberal clergywoman friend pause about her own unconditional acceptance of a woman's right to choose. To use paradigm language, this conservative radical used information the other side may have overlooked.

These examples do not compare in profundity with Nicodemus's encounter with Jesus, the Master Teacher. It is well to remember, however, that we can learn in unlikely places, including in the camp of the "enemy." It is usually unsettling to leave the safety of your own group filled with persons who think as you do, and go among persons who think differently. Furthermore, other members of your group are not necessarily pleased to see you go into the other camp. They, too, are uneasy that a different perspective might bring new insights that do not fit the accepted reasoning of the faction they represent in a theological or ideological conflict. It is not too far-fetched to assume that Nicodemus may have had this kind of uncertainty, because we are told that he did not go see Jesus in broad daylight but went by night (John 3:2). Perhaps he did not want his friends to know he was associating with this rabble-rouser.

We assume Nicodemus loved his community of faith deeply. Like us he must have believed in institutionalized religion, supported it with his time, his money, and his talent. He was even willing to defend it when it was under attack by outsiders. Committed and faithful as he was, Nicodemus must have harbored doubts about some religious thinking and patterns of behavior that needed to be reexamined and revitalized. His concerns were much like the ones we have about our church today, including the ones discussed in this book. He believed this man Jesus knew what needed to be done.

So we, with Nicodemus, go off into the night to meet Jesus. On his arrival Nicodemus acknowledged that Jesus was a teacher sent from God and asked Jesus to teach him. What happened next is what happens to us over and over again. Jesus taught but Nicodemus did not understand. Born again? "How can a man be born when he is old? Can he enter a second time into his mother's womb and be born?" (John 3:4). So Jesus tried again. He explained that being born again is starting over in a new way, under-standing differently than you ever have before. Nicodemus still did not comprehend the meaning of being "born of water and the Spirit" (John 3:5). He asked again, "How can this be?" (John 3:9). By now Jesus was becoming impatient and asked, "Are you a teacher of Israel, and yet you do not understand this?" (John 3:10).

We could interpret Nicodemus's lack of comprehension as plain stupidity. Plenty of us can identify with that! However, another interpretation seems more likely. His lack of understanding may not have been so much a mat-ter of failing to comprehend the concept of rebirth as his objection to the practicality of it. Nicodemus may well have understood Jesus. Unless you start over with a new spirit as well as new understanding, you will not succeed. Translated into today's situation, his objections might have been about two different issues. First, Nicodemus may have objected to the extremism of the suggestion. Starting over means discarding the old. Was Jesus saying there is no sense tinkering with the old system in order to effect transformation? Will God not be satisfied with a few little adjustments to one's life or to the way established religion does business? Must we be made *new,* be born *again,* set different priorities? That sounds so difficult it seems impossible! Yet that is what Jesus is demanding.

Second, Nicodemus's inability to believe rather than to understand Jesus may have stemmed from his exhaustion. If he were experiencing anxiety and disillusionment, he may have lacked the energy for the hard work required to start over. Jesus was asking a man of status to become a new person, to become as sensitive to the hurts of others as if learning of them for the first time. If Nicodemus's journey was much like ours, he probably thought Jesus was asking too much of him. He was an established religious leader who was already working long and hard for what he believed was right. How could God ask any more of him? How can he ask us for more? Must we start over with the same enthusiasm and hope we had when we were young and naïve, believing all things were possible? In today's world not only those of us who are old seem discouraged. Many young people as well seem disillusioned and unable to believe that transformation is possible. We seem resigned to the pragmatic fact that environmental destruction, racism, war and violence, poverty and despair are permanent conditions. Nicodemus's encounter with Jesus reminds us that it takes courage as well as conviction to believe that changes can be made, and that it is possible for a person or a church to be born again.

Nicodemus may have been like many of us who mean so well and try so hard only to find that the utopian dream we envision as the kingdom of God has not come as fast or in the ways we expected. Sometimes things do not seem better at all, they seem worse. If Nicodemus was a victim of burnout two thousand years ago, his name is legion today. Clergy, public school teachers, social workers, and others in professions that seek to make a difference in people's lives face a daunting challenge. Yet as surely as Nicodemus with his failed comprehension walks with us, so does the Son of God. Rebirth truly *is* the gospel message, whether we understand the hopefulness and joy of the message or not. "The wind blows where it wills, and you hear the sound of it, but you do not know whence it comes or whither it goes" (John 3:8). God does break in on people's lives, sometimes when we least expect it. It can happen to you, it can happen to me, no matter how badly we have bungled things in the past or how discouraged we are.

COURAGE TO REBUILD

There was a teaching film used in hospice-worker training a number of years ago. One of its purposes was to illustrate the resilience of the human spirit. It comes to mind as a modern-day parable for the plight of American society today, including its churches. The film told the story of a small village in Wales. Oberfan was a typical Welch mining community—small drab houses, a few stores, a church, and an elementary school. Next to the town was a slag heap, the kind commonly seen in mining areas. It had been there for generations, scarcely noticed but gradually growing as the men of the village worked the mine. Then in the middle of one weekday morning the weight of the debris suddenly shifted the mound. For no apparent reason, and without any warning, the slag heap came roaring down into the village, crushing everything in its path. It covered the elementary school where every child of the village was in attendance. Virtually none of them survived.

Along with each family's individual grief over the loss of the children, the people of the village had to deal with the guilt all of them felt for participating in the building of the slag pile. The film does not include much material about outsiders, but we can be sure there were significant efforts to fix the blame. The mining company may have been asked to pay reparations for its negligence in not providing safe storage for the debris. Government inspection laws were probably reviewed as everyone struggled to understand how this happened and who was to blame.

The story reminds me of the situation in which we find ourselves today as a nation and as the church. Though our losses are not as dramatic or as sudden as the losses in Oberfan, many of us feel we have suffered significant loss. We feel as if a slag pile shifted and buried our national and religious optimism. We are anxious to place blame. Conservatives blame liberals for the erosion of family values. Liberals blame conservatives for a climate of dogmatism and mean-spiritedness. Whites blame persons of color for taking more than their share. Nonwhites blame whites for not giving enough. All of us blame the establishment, the bureaucratic institutions that order our corporate life: schools, government, and churches.

Probably there is some truth in all of the accusations we hurl at each other. But we, like the citizens of Oberfan, must also come to grips with our own duplicity and guilt. The grandfathers and fathers of the village who dug the coal and added debris to the slag pile needed to acknowledge their role. The mothers and grandmothers who watched it grow without thinking of the consequences had to acknowledge their role. Each of us has stood by and watched the environment deteriorate, urban decay grow, racial tension escalate, our churches leave the inner cities, the influence of mainstream churches erode. We each played a role in creating our slag heap, and we need to own it. Sometime, in the personal and corporate lives of all of us, there comes a day of reckoning. A day when, without warning, the consequences of our actions or lack of action come roaring down upon us and destroy a precious gift, perhaps our children. After we have felt the guilt and fixed the blame we, like the citizens of Oberfan, must forgive ourselves and one another and start building again.

The film about Oberfan ends with footage of the children's Christmas program in the new school. All the young people of the village are on stage. There are little ones in the front rows and high school students behind them. One sees the noticeable gap of children in the middle range of ages. That group was lost, but the village goes on and so does the singing.

SUMMARY

This book contains some harsh words, but its intent is hopeful. Members of the Christian community cannot solve the church's problems by blaming one another. The divisiveness among and between our own members is a pivotal problem that must not be overlooked. As I have argued all through the book, each person and each faction within the community needs to listen to others more carefully. There is an urgent need for humility and lack of dogmatism on all our parts. None of us have the whole truth.

Each of us must assume responsibility for contributing to the situation in which we find ourselves. If we are to solve our problems we must ask penetrating questions about our predicament. Here I have tried to offer examples of possible questions about values, about the conflict between liberal and conservative Christians, about the racial conflict, and about the relevance of restructuring our religious bureaucracies. I urge readers to ask even better questions. Yet all our analysis will be doomed to failure if we do not heed the words spoken to Nicodemus. "Unless one is born of water and the Spirit, he cannot enter the kingdom of God" (John 3:5).

Not long ago Teresa Fry Brown left her pastoral assignment in the African Methodist Episcopal Church in Denver to become the first African American woman on the faculty of the Candler School of Theology in Atlanta. It was an exciting but risky decision to leave the security of a well-known world and move into unfamiliar territory. Let these words she spoke at a farewell dinner for family and friends be our response to the coming days within the church:

Hope is hearing the song of the future.
Faith is the courage to dance to it.

May we hear the song and find the courage to join the dance.

FOR REFLECTION

1. Have you ever begun a project with high hopes only to become discouraged and disappointed with the results? How did it make you feel?

2. Tell about an experience you have had with an "enemy" who turned out to be a more likable person than you expected.

3. Have you ever failed at something and decided to start over? What made you try again?